The World Is My Oyster

Volume 1

Matthias Drawe

Editor: René Alfaro

Cover image licensed from: ©
Shutterstock.com (ID: 68735026)
Photos in text: © Matthias Drawe or ©
Shutterstock.com

D.A. Publishing
228 Park Ave S #24579
New York, NY 10003
Tel.: +1-212-486-8049
info@da-publishing.com

ISBN: 9798706110284

CONTENTS

1. FELIZ NATAL – Christmas in Rio

Renzo and I walk along Copacabana beach. It's raining like hell and getting dark. If we hadn't taken the beach umbrella from his apartment, we'd be soaking wet by now.

Renzo is Italian and my neighbor. Being in his mid-thirties and short, he has buck teeth and a hook nose with a bluish spot right on the tip of the hook. He reminds me of Roberto Benigni. He's not exactly an Adonis but charming. Women like him.

Renzo knows almost everyone in Copacabana, and everyone knows him. He has been coming to Rio for ten years. Eight months a year he works on a merchant ship, the remaining four, he spends his money in Copacabana.

"I've been working on ships since I was seventeen," Renzo says. "I've been almost anywhere in the world. Singapore, Java, Borneo, Yokohama, San Francisco, Los Angeles, all of South America. But when I came to Rio, I knew right away: This is it! This is where I want to stay."

The beach promenade is deserted. All kiosks are closed. A lone jogger moves through the rain, and some homeless people seek shelter under an open-air stage.

Copacabana at dusk

It's not only the rain that's to blame for the somber atmosphere. Even in the rain there's always something going on at the beach promenade. Crowds make their way along the brightly lit Avenida Atlântica, past elegant hotels, expensive apartment buildings and restaurants. Street vendors offer their goods, performance artists try to earn a little change, and spontaneous parties happen on the beach. Virtually nonstop, 364 days a year. Just not today, because today is …

Christmas.

Christmas in Rio. The only day when everything is different. All shops and restaurants are closed.

"You can feel Christmas far in advance here," Renzo says. "On the beach, you see girls in bikinis wearing red and white Santa hats, and you see cashiers wearing them in the supermarket. It's the most important holiday in Brazil. All families are at home. You can feel it here more than in Europe, more than in the US, more than anywhere else. Everything is closed."

We tried to flag down a cab, but they are all taken. Some people in passing cars throw us curious glances: two gringos carrying a beach umbrella in the pouring rain on Avenida Atlântica.

A young Brazilian woman lowers her car window and sends us a kiss: *"Feliz Natal!"*

Renzo sends her a kiss back. *"Feliz Natal!"*

I'm exhausted since we've been walking for quite a while, now. Renzo points to the final stretch of Copacabana. "It's back there", he says. "We'll just have to keep walking a bit."

The only place open today is called Bei Willi, and it's a German pub. That's definitely not how I had imagined Christmas in Rio, but Renzo assures me that Bei Willi is totally cool, and anyways, we would have no other choice.

The place is a blend of a German pub and a Brazilian beach kiosk: massive wooden tables and huge beer mugs combined with palm fronds and bamboo shelves. The Brazilian flag flies next to the banner of the St. Pauli football club, and German pop songs alternate with Samba. There's a plastic Christmas tree, and colorful balloons float under the ceiling. At the buffet, a pork roast is being served.

The crowd matches the furnishings and the music. About twenty German men mingle with Brazilian *mulatas*. Some have taken to the small dancefloor in the far corner of the room.

Willi is behind the bar and pours beer. Being tall and skinny, he sports a perm. The gaze from his blue eyes is cold. He used to be a car dealer in Hamburg. At some point, he called it quits, took out his savings and stayed in Rio for good.

At once, Ana Luisa appears. Drunk.

"Brazil is great," she says, "simply the most beautiful country in the world. Sure, we have a few tiny problems, but people are happy anyway. Everyone is happy, right?"

Ana Luisa wears a Santa hat and a tight-fitting blouse with red wine stains. She has enormous boobs, and her slightly transparent blouse barely leaves anything to the imagination. In the US she would probably be arrested for indecent exposure in this outfit, but here it's quite normal.

Ana Luisa is a looker. A classic Brazilian mix: white, indigenous and black. Of her two children, one is from a Dane the other from a German. She lives with her mom, and today of all days they got into an argument. Willi was her last resort.

Ana Luisa is so drunk that she has trouble keeping her balance. When sloshed, she always talks about how beautiful Brazil is, says Renzo. She lived in Europe for a few years, but ended up feeling depressed.

Despite economic woes and poverty in plain sight, almost everyone here is a patriot and infectiously happy-go-lucky. A dash of occasional melancholy creeps in, but it comes rather from exhaustion after too much samba and booze. As soon as the body recovers, the party keeps going.

Renzo points to the young Brazilian women sitting at the tables. "They became moms at the tender age of fifteen or sixteen. And none are married, because Brazilian men, uh... they love to play around, but marriage ... not so much."

Willi plays a Christmas song: "Silent Night, Holy Night." In German. He hands out sparklers, and the German-Brazilian crowd waves them around.

Isabel, one of the girls at the next table, settles down with us. Her dark skin contrasts against a white tank top bearing the slogan: *No stress!* She wears tight-fitting hot pants and dizzying platform shoes.
"*Quatro bambini,*" whispers Renzo. "Four children!"

Isabel has a marked overbite and a receding chin. Her gelled, black hair shines in the light of the sparklers. She wants to know where I come from.

"Mexico," Renzo says.

He likes to introduce me as a Mexican because I speak Spanish, and this almost counts as Portuguese. Germans and Americans are not very popular in Rio because of communication barriers. Mexicans are cool, though.

"Mexico?" Isabel looks at me in disbelief. It seems she's trying to recognize the Mexican in my facial features. Ana Luisa also scans my face. Suddenly she lifts her glass but spills almost half of it as she makes another red wine stain on her blouse. *"Feliz Natal e viva México!"*

The next morning.

I'm at the beach, sitting in my folding chair, enjoying the sun. I've been in Rio for a week now and made it to a somewhat decent tan. At least I am not as pale as when I arrived.

I sip some coconut water to get over my Christmas hangover. It's supposed to be one of the best cures. I might have to drink another one since I don't feel being cured at all.

The beach teems with street vendors, and some

guys play volleyball. I notice the beach cops. I've never seen such good-looking cops. Their uniforms consist of skin-tight undershirts, shorts and cool sunglasses. And they are toned to a T of course. No wonder there's always a fan club of beach hotties around them.

Actually, one might think that this is a dream job, but the pay is not that impressive. They earn about 250 dollars a month.

Renzo and Ana Luisa show up. She spent the night with him.

Ana Luisa and Renzo at the beach

While Renzo heads to one of the beach kiosks to get drinks, Ana Luisa massages her temples, her face slightly puffy.

She has this melancholic look that Brazilians often have in the morning. Although she usually talks a lot, she's quiet now. Maybe she thinks about her kids. In Brazil, the presents are hidden under the bed and given on the morning of Christmas Day. But going home for Ana Luisa is no option. The family fight last night was too ugly.

She stares at the ocean. "New Year's Eve in Rio. A wild party. Mark my words. All people clad in white. I don't even know exactly why. I think it means peace."

Renzo comes back with a coconut and a can of beer. Ana Luisa opens the can and downs it in one swig. "Breakfast beer," she says with a grin. She gives Renzo a kiss. *"Obrigado, meu amor."*

They are cuddling up. A popular sport in Rio. I've never seen so many couples kissing in public. It starts at adolescence and there's no age limit. Even people past eighty still kiss in the open. Always and everywhere. Maybe it's something in the water. It's certainly nice to look at: Love is in the air.

I spot a beach beauty wearing a white, pointed hat with gilded lettering: *Feliz Reveillon* – Happy New Year. A few other girls also don the white hats. It's crazy, yesterday was Christmas with Santa hats, and now we are basically at New Year's already.

An older man points to Ana Luisa's empty beer can. "Can I have it?"

"Sure!" She throws it into a plastic bag, home to several hundred other cans. The man carries the outsized bag on his back as he walks on. He'll get a couple of *centavos* for each can.

A bit later we are in Tabajaras, a favela that sits right behind Copacabana. Carlos, Ana Luisa's cousin, lives here. He and his wife provide a laundry service which comes a lot cheaper than going to the laundromat.

The TV is running in the living room. While sleeping, they might turn it off but otherwise, it's a constant companion.

While Carlos's wife takes care of our laundry, we drink Brazilian red wine from a gallon-sized bottle. It's sweet and not really up my ally, but I drink it anyway.

Carlos resembles Ana Luisa. He's also a mix of white, indigenous and black. Dark-brown skin, almond eyes, slightly curly hair. He wears shorts, flip flops and no shirt, like most men in the favela in this scorching heat. The left half of his face has been paralyzed after a car accident.

Favela in Rio de Janeiro

Occasionally some children run through the living room and across the yard. Carlos has four kids, though he is only twenty-eight. His neighbor has five.

There's a game show on TV. The host's assistant is a Brazilian blonde with impressive curves. She wears a tiny string bikini which is called *fio dental* – dental floss – because it leaves little to the imagination. The beauty's largest garment is a transparent veil over her face.

Carlos points out that the lady's breasts and her bottom are silicone-reinforced. It's not really clear why she wears the veil, but it looks good on her. It gives her a certain touch of mystery.

The home is well equipped: a massive fridge, a gas stove with six burners, a substantial sound system, and a clunky laptop. It's not top of the line, but the essentials are covered.

The outside walls of the house haven't been plastered and show crude clay bricks, but on the inside it's neat and cozy. A common sight in a favela. All that matters is the inside.

Half an hour later, we are back on the street with our laundry, waiting for the *transporte alternativo*, a privately-run van, which shuttles back and forth in the favela. It stops wherever someone signals.

The favelas in Copacabana are situated on the steep hills that border the borough. The makeshift houses are perched on the hills.

It started long ago in the 1940s, and it's all illegal, but the government decided to just ignore it. The favelas have become so vast that a third of Rio's population are favela dwellers.

Favelas are basically lawless areas. There are some self-appointed community associations who keep informal property records, but order is maintained by the drug cartels. People say that nobody steals in a favela because the gangsters are more efficient than the police. If they catch a thief, they break his arm.

Usually, there's just one paved access road from which the homes can be reached via narrow alleys and stairs. The people who live high up are the poorest, because it's inconvenient. The only access are steep stairs. Try to deliver a fridge there. Or building material.

But in this case, there's an upside for the poor: They have an ocean view! And their kids look fantastically healthy because they climb the stairs every day.

The van doesn't really have a schedule, and we are still waiting for it at the access road. Maybe it broke down somewhere. A few men drink beer in front of a small bodega, a mangy dog limps across the street and two boys play ball. It's almost like in a village. You get the feeling that everyone knows everyone.

Two letters, however, signal that things are not always as calm as they seem. The letters *C.V.* are spray-painted on several walls. They stand for *Comando Vermelho* – Red Command. It's the sign of a drug cartel that controls this favela. Anyone selling drugs here who is not a member of the *Comando Vermelho* will be killed.

The next morning.

Renzo is at his window, smoking a cigarette. Our vacation rentals are next to each other and when looking out the window, we can shake hands. We rented our furnished one-room apartments from an agency. I pay thirty dollars a day, Renzo only twenty. Our apartments are practically identical, but Renzo haggled like a madman and got a better deal.

I didn't' take too well to that red wine in the favela and have a headache.
"What time is it?"
"Don't know," Renzo says. "Does it matter?"
"No, not really."
I'm searching my luggage for some aspirin. The furnishings of my apartment have the charm of the seventies. The stereo and the TV look as if they were imported ages ago from a communist Eastern European country. The bookshelf indicates that legions of travelers have passed through. The jetsam they left behind consists of titles like: *Buddhism for Beginners*, *Love Story* (in French) and a political manifesto by Rush Limbaugh, entitled: *The Way Things Ought to Be*.

Renzo and I are having lunch. There's a small restaurant on our street where we can sit outside. The tables and chairs display the logo of a beer brand. Dried fish dangle from a beam, and two cab drivers are having a quick coffee at the bar. The food is very affordable. A steak with potatoes and a large bottle of local beer will set you back about five bucks.

The big Brazilian beer brands are called *Skol*, Swedish for "Cheers", *Antarctica*, and *Brahma*. It's not clear to me what Brazilian beer has to do with Sweden, the Antarctic or a Hindu god, but it's not that important. All perfectly fine, as long as it's cold.

The restaurant has two wall clocks. One above the entrance to the bathroom and one behind the bar. One shows 9:15 a.m., the other 2:40 p.m.

Question: Which one shows the right time?

Answer: Both are wrong.

Even the digital clocks on the beach promenade don't show accurate time. There's a lack of maintenance, and nobody really cares anyway.

"Time is a relative term here," Renzo says. "It doesn't matter what day it is, Monday, Tuesday, Wednesday, whether it's five, six or two in the morning. It doesn't matter because there's always something going on around here."

Renzo is right. Rio has already sucked me in. The first day, I went to bed early because of exhaustion from the flight, but since my second day, it's been a constant party. I forgot what day of the week it is and don't wear my wristwatch anymore.

A little boy, about eight years old, appears next to us and points to the leftovers on our plates. He is barefoot and wears only shorts. Renzo signals the waiter to bring a disposable plate to collect the leftovers. The boy nods silently and leaves with the food. After a few steps, he greedily stuffs it into his mouth.

December 31st.

The party starts in the late afternoon. Samba bands parade along the beach promenade, followed by thousands of dancers. It's raining again, but nobody seems to care.

Renzo grabs me by the arm and pulls me right into the crowd. At first, I dance rather reserved, but slowly I get the knack of it and start to merge with the rhythm.

Renzo has closed his eyes and fidgets ecstatically back and forth. He's a little off the beat, but that doesn't matter here.

"Feliz ano novo!" Isabel, the girl from the German pub, suddenly hugs me and gives me a wet kiss that tastes of apple cider. As if by divine intervention, Isabel and Ana Luisa have been dancing in the samba crowd we just joined.

Each year, more than two million people celebrate New Year's in Copacabana. We can hardly move, because everybody wants to see the fireworks. Several ocean liners float about a mile off the beach. The passengers will watch the fireworks from the sea.

The author in the New Year's bustle

There are people hugging and kissing all over the place. Most of them wear white outfits, soaked by the rain. The wet clothes become transparent and some women seem almost naked. Right next to us, there's a group of a hundred young gays who are hugging and kissing.

Renzo has Ana Luisa in his arms and yells: *"Feliz ano novo!"*

Isabel offers me a sip from her bottle of apple cider. She wishes me *"Saude, paz e dinheiro!"* – Health, peace and money!

I'm already quite sloshed. Starting in the afternoon, Renzo and I have guzzled quite a few beers, spiked by an occasional *caipirinha*.

"Why didn't you wish for *amor?*"

"Pardon?" – Isabel doesn't understand what I mean.

I want to know why she wished for health, peace and money, but not love?

Isabel laughs and spreads her arms: "Love? Look around you! – We have enough of that!"

Isabel and I throw white orchids into the sea. I bought the flowers for the insane price of ten dollars. As we approach midnight, they get more expensive by the minute.

Thousands of flowers float in the sea, and each and every one of them is a wish for the New Year. Some people even walk into water. It's a bit dangerous, because the waves are quite high.

Renzo and Ana Luisa have disappeared in the crowd. There's little chance of finding them again in this hustle and bustle.

Fireworks in Copacabana

"*Vamos!*" – Isabel drags me into the sea. We're already wet from the rain, so what the heck. We frolic around in the lukewarm ocean just like the people next to us. It's a lot of fun, and I almost feel like a kid jumping around in a puddle. But suddenly, a strong wave takes us off our feet and washes us onto shore. We laugh and hug, and at once, we're kissing. It's true. There's plenty of love in Rio.

First of January in the afternoon.

"Porca Madonna!" Renzo swears at the ATM, because his account is maxed out.

I check my account. Just like Renzo, I'm almost broke. The machine only gives me twenty bucks. I kept doling out my money in Rio and didn't even want to think about the balance.

Renzo and I settle down in the sand on the beach and drink canned beer from the supermarket. We stare at the ocean in silence. As always, crowds of tourists stroll along the beach promenade. Some people dance to the music from a loudspeaker, and street vendors try to peddle their wares: sunglasses, grilled shrimps on skewers, beach towels ...

Renzo fishes his last cigarette out of the pack. I've never seen him so quiet. The blue spot on his hooked nose looks darker than usual today. Tomorrow, he must get back on a ship. It will take weeks until he reaches the next port.

"Hey," Renzo says. "We haven't exchanged addresses yet." He asks for something to write at a beach kiosk and scribbles his info on a napkin. "I'll be back in a few months. Maybe you'll come by to join me."

A few days later, I'm back home in wintry New York. On a cold evening, I hear familiar sounds on the street. The thickly wrapped people in front of me – two men and a woman – speak Portuguese. They seem to have just arrived, dragging their suitcases behind them. As they turn around to check a street sign, I see their dark brown faces. They move awkwardly in their winter clothes and stand out in snowy New York. Just like the pale gringos did in Copacabana.

2. HELSINKI CONFIDENTIAL – A look behind the scenes in the Finnish capital

The guy next to me at the bar has been staring at the wall for over half an hour. His mouth is slightly agape, his gaze blank. Occasionally he takes a sip of beer.

I've noticed this gaze in other men around here. I've seen it in a streetcar and in the waiting room at the harbor where the ferries leave for the islands. It's an empty stare without focus. Later I will learn that this gaze is a classic and even has a name.

But we're not quite there yet.

Finland achieved considerable prosperity and has one of the best education systems in the world, despite the fact that it's far off the beaten track and has a language that hardly anyone understands. Except for the Finns of course.

My editor at the radio station paid for my flight. He discovered that the human-interest department hadn't reported about Finland since 1959 and asked me if I wanted to do a story. Condition: I need to go to

Helsinki in the dead of winter. How does it feel to live in this freezing, gloomy weather with only a few hours of daylight?

Downtown Helsinki in winter

So here I am in Helsinki in the midst of winter, having a drink at a bar that's attached to a community theatre. Through a friend, I got in touch with Erkki Hämäläinen, an actor. I'm crashing on his couch. Erkki is a jolly fellow and always open for international visitors. His last name is a riot: three umlaut *A*s and an *I* after the last umlaut. Where else can you find a name like this?

Today is the opening night of a new play. An experiment. Erkki and his colleagues are excited and caught up in the final preparations.

Both, the theater and the bar, are sponsored by the government. Therefore, the prices are more moderate than elsewhere but still quite steep. Helsinki is expensive. Very expensive. Especially booze. Nevertheless, people drink with a vengeance. But how can they afford it at these prices? It won't take long until I'll find out.

But we're not quite there yet.

My gazing neighbor turns to me with a sudden resolve. "You know what …?"
He must have ingested quite a bit of fuel already, swaying slightly on his bar stool. He takes a deep breath. What does he want to say? His gaze is a bit shrouded. Then he lets it out:

"Existentialism is bullshit!"

Wow. Quite a powerful statement. I search for a philosophical riposte, but my new buddy doesn't even want to hear it. He orders a double vodka and stares at the wall again. Later I will learn that there's a phenomenal Finnish joke on the subject, a joke which made me laugh so hard that my belly hurt.

But we're not quite there yet.

I look at my watch. Close to eight. The play is about to start! I head to the lobby. A long line has formed in front of the box office.
Apparently, there's a strong appreciation for culture in Helsinki. Outside, it's about minus ten Fahrenheit. You really must be a theater lover to venture out in this weather. On the other hand: Minus ten is probably wussy stuff for a real Finn. A Finn

doesn't feel the cold. Only wimpy Southerners like me get the shivers.

I have a cool VIP ticket, and my seat is right at the front. As a journalist, I get special treatment. Sweet! At first, I was slightly afraid that I might understand zilch if everything is in Finnish, but Erkki reassured me that I'll understand as much as everyone else. The play uses *Grammelot*, a kind of fantasy language. The actors speak emotional gibberish along with expressive gestures.

The curtain rises. The stage is completely empty. No stage design, nothing. Not even a chair. Pretty impressive …

Orchestral music sets in that hints at danger. Two actors rush onto the stage. They are dressed all in black and obviously have a problem.

Erkki and Minna on stage

They are being chased and must escape. Fear of death. An epic theme. The fear is palpable, even if the actors speak gibberish. There's only one way out. But it's very dangerous since it leads across an abyss …

Unfortunately, the *Grammelot* concept is exhausted after twenty minutes. One emotion follows another, and there's no discernible plot. Or maybe there is one, but it doesn't become clear.

I sneak out to the bathroom. Would be a tough call to be glued into the theater seat for another hour of *Grammelot*.

I settle down at the bar again. The anti-existentialist is still staring at the wall. Pretty consistent.

The bar is packed, even though the play is on. Apparently, the art isn't that important, but the government-sponsored prices are.

Most of the patrons don't seem to be artsy types at all. The women wear preppy outfits, and some men are dressed in suits and ties. The atmosphere is extremely soft. No one yells or gets loud, and the background music is smooth.

But then, a woman gets up, heads to the next table and repeatedly and forcefully hits a guy with her handbag. Without a word she sits down again, and everyone continues talking as before.

I look at the philosopher at my side. No reaction. He keeps staring at the wall. He must have noticed the incident, but apparently it doesn't trigger any reaction in him.

I ask the bartender. "What was that?"

"Little argument between former lovers. It builds up and has to get out somehow."

"No words at all?"

"Why? The handbag says it all."

"Does this sort of thing happen often?"

The bartender nods. The Finns are obviously sparing with words but still quite emotional. Except you wouldn't know it by looking at them. Finnish temperament takes a while to build.

I hear applause. The play is over. Sneaking back into the theater, I clap along and head backstage to the premiere party.

Erkki wants to know how I liked the play.

"Very powerful," I say. Okay, it's a little white lie, but I am Erkki's guest and don't want to hurt him. Besides, I'm not a theater critic. If I were, I'd probably tell him that a gibberish play carries twenty minutes at most.

"Okay", Erkki says. "Let's go to the sauna."

"Sauna?"

"Yes, my friend. You are in Finland, now!"

The theater has its own sauna, and the opening party is held there. A few minutes later, the actors and I sit naked in the sauna surrounded by steam. Everyone drinks beer. Standard procedure. In Finland people also drink in the sauna. Someone brought a bottle of vodka and we kick back shots.

Erkki starts singing. Judging from his gestures, it's a love song. Cheers from the crowd.

I glance at the actresses. I really like Minna. Erkki told me that she's single. Good to know. After all, she might be interested in a foreign journalist ...

After the sauna, the party continues. We head to a tango bar. Finnish tango. The music sounds like Argentine tango, but the lyrics are in Finnish.

I had no idea that there was tango in Finland, but the tradition is almost a hundred years old and has been kept alive to this very day.

Erkki says that he's not into tango, but that he wanted to show me what else there is in Helsinki. Minna, on the other hand, knows how to tango, and takes the opportunity to sway across the dancefloor.

Finnish tango

The tango place closes at midnight and we move to a techno disco. The music is really loud and it's impossible to communicate. We dance. Techno is not really my thing, but I jump around on the dance floor anyway. In the strobe light, it doesn't matter whether you got rhythm or not.

The disco closes at 2 a.m. As we head outside, I notice a guy in a park sitting all alone on a fifteen-feet-high rock formation. He's only wearing a T-shirt and sings a Finnish song. At ten below zero! Erkki says that this is normal. Finns simply like to sing.

No one wants to go home, but everything's closed by now. Erkki suggests that we have tea at his apartment. Finnish tradition. To wrap up the evening, you drink some tea.

Shortly after, we sit in a circle on the carpeted floor in Erkki's living room. Apart from Erkki and me, there are Minna, Agneta and Mikka – all of them actors from the play.

I don't know why we sit on the floor, but maybe it's also a Finnish tradition. And of course, the tea isn't just tea. It's spiked with booze. Right then, I discover the little secret why the Finns can afford the horrendous prices in bars. They all have a bottle of high-proof hidden in their bags. Even the women! They occasionally refuel in the restroom, so the bill won't get out of proportion.

What is it about that empty gaze that I've noticed all around? My new friends smirk. They all know it of course. They explain that the gaze is called *Finnish stare*. It's usually seen in men who drink a lot and delve deep into their thoughts. There's even a joke on the subject, and Erkki tells it like this:

Two Finns are sitting across from each other in a gloomy bar, drinking vodka. They don't look at each other but stare at the table. Apart from them, there's only the innkeeper. It's quiet. No music, no one says a word.

Both guys kick back their vodka. The innkeeper appears and fills the glasses to the brim again.

The guys compose themselves for a moment, kick back the vodka and stare at the table. It's quiet. No one says a word. The host appears again and pours more vodka.

One of the guys suddenly raises his glass and says: "Cheers!"

Replies the other: "Wait a minute! — You want to talk, or you want to drink?"

I can hardly contain myself and laugh like crazy. But maybe it's so funny because I've already guzzled a whole lot of spiked tea.

Mikka starts singing in Finnish. He has a beautiful voice. Seems to be a rather sad song. The others have moist eyes.

Agneta lightens the mood, as she sings a drinking song. The others join in, and I clap along. The crowd decides that it's my turn, now.

I rarely sing, but what the heck. I need to deliver something. Because of the spiked tea, my inhibitions are pretty low anyway. A song comes to mind that I once learned as a teenager. The melody isn't that challenging, so I might be able to nail it. I start to sing:

You are my sunshine, my only sunshine,
You make me happyyyy, when skies are grey,
You never know, dear, how much I love you,
Please don't take my sunshine away-hay …

The others remain silent. Did I hit a wrong note? Erkki pats my back. "Welcome to Finland. That wasn't so bad!"

We continue drinking spiked tea, chatting and singing. Or to be more exact: I let the others sing and clap along. As the night advances, I notice that Mikka's gaze turns blank. The Finnish stare! Shortly after, he gets up and staggers toward the bathroom. The others look exhausted as well. They get up one after the other and walk towards the bathroom. No one comes back.

Eventually, I need the bathroom, too. The door is open. No one inside. Where are they? I relieve myself and peek into the kitchen. Mikka is sitting at the table, sleeping. His head has sunk to the tabletop. Agneta is across from him, sleeping in a similar position.

The door to Erkki's bedroom is open. He's on his bed fully dressed, all fours stretched out. Minna has fallen asleep in Erkki's armchair, her head tilted back. She snores. Since they didn't come back to the living room, I thought that there was some hanky-panky going on, but it seems like they've just collapsed from exhaustion.

I head back to the living room and crash on the couch. In the middle of the night, I come to with infernal thirst and stagger into the kitchen. Agneta and Mikka have disappeared. There's a water bottle in the fridge, but it's empty. I guzzle some tap water. It tastes funny, but I keep drinking anyway.

Erkki's still stretched out on his bed and snores. Minna has left.

When I wake up the next day, it's four o'clock in the afternoon and already dark. Helsinki has only a few hours of daylight in winter. I've missed an entire day!

It smells of coffee. Erkki is in the kitchen, having breakfast. He reads the reviews for the theater premiere. Most of the reactions are positive, Erkki says, but generally the critics think the play is a bit too long.

I have some coffee and scrambled eggs. Erkki brought water, and I kill an entire bottle. I don't feel that great, but it could be worse.

What shall we do with the rest of the day? Erkki says, he needs a break and will stay at home. – Okay, so we're staying at home, recharging the battery.

Erkki reads a book, and I settle down on my couch and turn on the TV. It's a pretty old thing, and Erkki only has the channels that are free. My options: a news program, a documentary about whaling and ice hockey. I stick with ice hockey. It's relaxing because you don't have to think much. Even if you don't speak Finnish, everything is crystal clear: Two teams are chasing a puck, trying to get it into the opponent's goal. Wonderful. Just what I need right now.

Ice hockey is almost a religion in Finland. Soccer

doesn't count, only ice hockey is really important. There's one thing that you must not mention under any circumstances: Never say that the puck is hard to follow because it's so small. This could hurt a Finn to the bone and destroy a friendship forever.

The game on TV seems to be an important match. The announcer is quite animated and even screams occasionally. The players tackle their opponents mercilessly and smash them against the side boundaries. I sense that there's real passion at play here. But where's that dang puck again? Well, somehow, it's not that important. You can guess where it is because that's where they're all heading when it slides into a far corner.

Occasionally, they show close-ups, and you can feel that the game is a lot of fun despite the tough fight.

Good vibes at the game

I head to the kitchen to brew some tea. But this time, I won't spike it. The door to Erkki's room is open. He's reading Sartre. In Finnish. Sartre was not only a philosopher but also a playwright, of course, and I thought that Erkki would read one of the plays but far from it. He reads Sartre's main philosophical work: *Being and Nothingness.*

It's existentialism, of course. I learned that at some point in college. But the details? Right off the bat, I only remember one term: *Being-for-itself.* It's very important and basically the crucial point. Meaning? Well, it was a long time ago. I'd have to look it up.

Erkki says that the first ten pages are quite complex and that he's already read them four times. But he definitely wants to continue. He's determined to finish every book he starts.

I remember the guy from the bar. The one with the Finnish stare. He also mentioned existentialism. Perhaps Sartre is hip in Finland right now. Actually, it's been seventy years since existentialism was hip, but maybe it's because Sartre has only now been translated into Finnish. It's possible that *Being and Nothingness* arrived in Finland only after a seventy-year delay. Or: The first translation was bad, and only now a good one has come out.

My hangover is acting up, and I'd rather not think about it any further. All I need is a good cup of hot tea!

I'm back on the couch, watching ice hockey and drinking tea. Ah, it's great! They're still running after the puck from one side of the rink to the other. Very calming. Absolutely zero mental effort. You just need to stare at the screen, so you don't miss a goal.

I wonder if there are any Finnish hockey players reading *Being and Nothingness*, now that there's a good translation. Probably not. A hockey player who reads Sartre would probably miss the puck at the crucial moment.

The game is over. A draw. Very nice. Now both teams have kind of won. I turn off the TV and hit the sack.

The next morning,

I wake up early. The sun shines through the living room window. Wow! I haven't seen the sun since I've arrived in Helsinki. I head outside. It's a wonderful day with crystal clear air. Helsinki is not very big, so I hop on a bus and venture into nature.

Landscape at the outskirts of Helsinki

The visuals are great, no question about it. What comes to mind? Sibelius, of course! He's Finland's most famous composer. I grab my phone and find his 5th Symphony online. Excellent. At once, it all makes sense: the cold, the snow, the saunas and the Finnish stare. If you listen closely to Sibelius, it's all there. Even the spiked tea.

After spending half an hour in the enchanting landscape, the cold creeps into my bones. My clothes are not weatherproof for Finland!

I hurry to the bus stop and head back to town. Today there's a team meeting in the theater. In the sauna. They're discussing the spring program. With beer and small appetizers on Finnish crispbread. As a foreign journalist, I'm invited and very much looking forward to it. It's so nice and warm!

3. HAITI, CHÉRIE – A country in turmoil

Jean-Robert races his rickety jeep through the narrow, bumpy streets of Port-au-Prince. He speeds up a steep hill. If he didn't know the back roads, we'd be screwed.

"That certain gentleman was a symbol for all Haitians," he says, referring to Jean-Bertrand Aristide. "We believed he was a disciple of Martin Luther King and Gandhi and that he was the solution to Haiti's problems, but he turned out to be the opposite."

A protest is marching through downtown Port-au-Prince. If we can't get to the bank in Pétion-Ville, we'll have a serious problem. Jean-Robert needs medicine for his daughter, and without cash I am doomed. Even in the hotel, I can't do without cash. The phone lines and the internet are down, and credit cards are worthless.

The trip to Haiti was an idea of the editor at my radio station. The country is constantly in the headlines, and he wanted a story.

Haiti is only a short flight from New York, and the room rate in my historic hotel is relatively cheap. Sixty bucks a night. It's a landmark with an interesting story and famed guests. But we'll get to this later.

The current situation in the country is precarious. There are clashes almost every day, and it can quickly turn dangerous.

Riots in Port-au-Prince

Jean-Robert tries to avoid the potholes but there are just too many. It's a bumpy ride. His glasses keep slipping off his nose, and he keeps pushing them up.

We pass a protest in front of us just in time and turn into the road to Pétion-Ville. The people on the street are clearly against the former beacon of hope. On almost every wall, I see the Creole graffiti *Aba Aristide!* – Down with Aristide!

"The biggest problem is that there's no health care," Jean-Robert says. "Most children don't go to school at all or not much longer than four years. And food is simply too expensive. At the same time, Aristide and his family fill their pockets."

Jean-Robert abruptly steps on the brakes, and the car comes to a screeching halt. The oncoming jeep almost collided head-on with us. The driver honks like a madman.

Jean-Robert cut a curve, and it was pure luck that we didn't collide with the other car. He quickly shifts into first gear and drives on. A woman, who had almost been pinned against a wall, yells a curse, and the driver of the jeep makes an obscene gesture in our direction.

Shortly after, we arrive in Pétion-Ville. Rich people and foreigners live in this upscale neighborhood that is perched on a hillside. We are looking for an American bank, but to our surprise, there's an empty lot where the bank used to be. The branch moved about two weeks ago, but nobody knows where to. Maybe they just called it quits and left the country.

It's Friday afternoon, and time is running out. We decide to try the National Bank of Haiti a few blocks down.

The bank is guarded by armed security personnel, and I'm searched for weapons. Jean-Robert stays behind in the car.

The interior of the bank is very clean and air conditioned. It feels like passing the barrier between the third and the first world. The Haitian employees are neatly dressed.

There are long lines in front of the tellers. I head to the info desk. Two Haitians in front of me have a problem with a check. It seems to be a serious problem because they're both upset. I fear that this could take a long time. Everything takes a long time in Haiti. A very long time.

But to my surprise, a manager approaches me – I am the only white person in the bank. I explain that I have an American account and need money.

"Do you have your passport with you, sir?"

I hand over my passport. He walks me to his desk and points to a card reader: "Slide the card through and enter your PIN."

My credit card is not in pristine condition. I had it in my back pocket for two days, hoping to pass an ATM somewhere, only to find out that there are no ATMs in Haiti. The card must have warmed in the sun and is slightly bent. To my surprise, it seems to work. The display shows a message: *Attendez s'il vous plaît.*

I wait.

For what seems like an eternity, nothing happens. Eventually, I get another message: *Carte invalide!* – Invalid card.

I try again. Same result. The manager shows me the way to the door.

Jean-Robert honks like a madman so that people let us through the street market. In the meantime, he found out the new address of Citibank. But to get there, we have to pass through the crowd.

The market is pure chaos. The tables are overloaded with pots, kettles, food, clothes. Some women hold out live chickens in front of them. They secure them by their feet, holding them upside down to paralyze them. Some merchants have laid out tarpaulins with goods right on the street, leaving only a narrow alley for traffic.

Street market in Port-au-Prince

Jean-Robert has no mercy. He honks incessantly, revs up the engine and pushes forward through the crowd. Some people leap out of the way, scared. A woman, who carries a heavy load on her head, also takes a leap, but miraculously keeps her balance.

As we make our way through the market, I notice curious glances. Whites are rare in Haiti. A girl touches my arm, which I have put on the ledge of the car window. Two little boys point their fingers at me and shout in Creole: *Blan, blan!* – A white guy, a white guy!

A few miles away people may die in the protest, but

there's no sign of it here. You'd never believe that some sort of civil war is raging close by.

Twenty minutes later.

The lady at the Citibank information desk looks at me with regret. *"Désolé, Monsieur,* I can't help you."

"But I have an account at Citibank, why can't I get any money?"

"We are Citibank Haiti, *Monsieur.* We are not linked to the American Citibank. You can only get money if you have a Haitian account."

The mood in the bank is not too good. It's terribly overcrowded, and people are trying to withdraw as much money as they can. I'm about to lose it. Finally, I made it into Citibank from which I can get money almost anywhere in the world. But not here.

"Two blocks away, there's an international ATM. Have you tried it?"

Is the information lady trying to get rid of me? I've heard that there's not a single ATM in all of Haiti, and now, one popped up just two blocks away? The gentleman behind me nods and confirms that the ATM exists. It's in the parking lot of a shopping center.

Shortly after, I'm in line at the ATM. It's the first and only ATM in all of Haiti at an upscale shopping center for the rich where you can buy imported luxury goods. Guards with machine guns secure the area.

The ATM is located at the back of the SOGE Bank, which has a branch in the building. The line advances rather slowly, but it moves. And there seems to be good news: The machine actually dispenses money.

Eventually, it's my turn and I cautiously feed my bent card into the slot. I'm afraid that the machine might simply swallow it. I've seen it happen to a guy in front of me. For whatever reason, the machine just sucked in his card. But mine seems to be fine. The machine asks for my PIN and the amount I want to withdraw. Everything goes smoothly until it comes to the withdrawal: *Nous sommes désolés. Cette transaction ne peut être conclue.*

"Merde alors!" I curse in French. The machine speaks French, so I somehow automatically replied in French.

I try again with a lower amount, only to be rejected again. The crowd behind me gets restless: *"Monsieur, s'il vous plaît,* there are also other people here!"

"Okay, okay, I'm done."

I give up. I knew right away that it wasn't gonna work.

Jean-Robert pours water on a napkin and wipes his forehead. He seems to have doubts about my financial prowess by now. I remember that I can get cash from an American Express office with a check and my passport. Jean-Robert gives me a tired look: *"Ça ne marche pas."*

He explains that the American Express office is on the other side of town, not far from the hotel. First of all, we probably wouldn't get through the protest and second of all, the office closes in twenty minutes.

"Why didn't you tell me that Amex was near the hotel?"

"You didn't ask me, you wanted to go to Citibank."

Jean-Robert has another idea. There's a Canadian Nova Scotia Bank nearby. He has heard that some foreigners were able to get money there. We must hurry, because Nova Scotia will also close in twenty minutes.

Jean-Robert races over a bumpy road. The door of the glove compartment pops open. He slams it shut, but soon after, it pops open again. Suddenly, the engine stutters and stops. We're out of gas. Jean-Robert emits an elaborate curse in Creole. I don't speak Creole, but it's close enough to French. As far as I can tell, there are whores involved, intimate body parts and even the devil.

The bank is about to close. Since the branch is only a few hundred yards away, I decide to run for it. It's hot and I'm soaked with sweat. The Haitians by the roadside smirk. One of them shouts in English: "Go, man, go!"

When I get to the branch, a bank clerk is just about to close the door. Again, there are armed guards at the entrance.

"Je vous en prie, Monsieur," I plead. *"Laissez moi entrer!"*

The guy seems to take pity and ushers me in. My hair is soaking wet, and sweat pours into my eyes.

There are still quite a few customers in the bank. On one side of the room, the lights are already switched off and the blinds have been lowered.

I head to the information desk and explain that I have an American account and want to withdraw 500 dollars.

The lady tells me that I have to pay 275 Haitian *gourdes* – about seven dollars – so she can make a phone call to Canada to verify my account. If something turns out to be wrong, the 275 *gourdes* will be lost. I fish a few bills out of my pocket. My last 400 *gourdes*.

The lady heads to the back area and dials a telephone number.

I close my eyes and collect myself. I have never been in such a chaotic country where almost nothing works. The roads are a nightmare, and there are power outages on a daily basis.

In my hotel, the hot water doesn't work. Just to get a simple cup of coffee in the restaurant takes about an hour. And they charge sixty bucks a day which is a huge sum in Haiti. Even stocking up on basic supplies seems to be a problem. Example:

"I'd like the avocado sandwich."

"Sorry, sir, we don't have any avocados right now."

"Okay, then I'll have a fruit salad."

"Just a minute, I need to check – Sorry, sir. Fruit will be delivered only tomorrow."

It's hard to explain. Haiti is a tropical country and avocados and fruit should be available in abundance.

"D'accord," the bank lady says and returns my passport. "Your account is fine. The fee for the transaction would be forty dollars."

"Okay." I don't care if the fee is insane, as long as I get my hand on some cash.

But there's a new hurdle: She tries to trace the raised numbers on my card with a mechanical credit card machine onto a carbon paper form. But since the plastic is bent, and the card doesn't fit neatly, the machine won't slide over it. The lady tries again, breaks her neatly manicured fingernail in the process and mumbles something in Creole.

I offer to press the card with both index fingers onto the pad while she slides the machine across. Together we slowly work our way forward. Eventually, the numbers appear on the carbon paper.

I receive a wait number and am ushered into the restricted area. There's a barred door, guarded by security personnel. In front of the door is a woman who has emptied the contents of her handbag on the floor: keys, sunglasses, a few crumpled banknotes, make-up utensils, a pack of tampons. Has she lost her wait number?

In the far corner of the corridor, I discover a

discarded door of a safe and a broken toilet bowl. I start to doubt that I will receive any money here.

But when it is my turn, the agent in the security area slides five hundred-dollar bills through the opening in the bullet-proof window. It's a surprise because up to now, I have only received money in the local currency abroad. Five hundred-dollar bills, of all things. I'd like to get it a bit smaller, but there is no change.

At once, I'm afraid that the bills might be counterfeit. Something similar happened to a friend of mine in Mexico. But there's no way I can check, and the bills look okay at first glance.

I head out. The money is in my underwear. Jean-Robert found a guy who'll tow us to the nearest gas station. The car pulling us with a flimsy rope is a jalopy of unknown make. Although we are on a relatively smooth road, it seems that this fossil constantly drives through potholes. The wheels are bent and wobble. In addition, the engine misfires and the exhaust emits a dark cloud of smoke. The rear window has a crack and is held together with a sticker which says: *Jesú est le sauveur* – Jesus is the savior.

We purchase half a gallon of gas with my last supply of Haitian *gourdes*. Nobody can break a hundred dollars of course.

Jean-Robert heads to the black market where we'll get forty-two *gourdes* for a dollar. In the hotel they only pay thirty-five. We stop at a run-down colonial-style house. Jean-Robert sounds the horn. A few seconds later, a guy shows up wearing a floppy hat that reads *Yogi Bear.*

I hand over two hundred dollars, and the guy checks the bills against the light. If it turns out that the bank slipped me counterfeit money, I'm screwed. Jean-Robert would probably strangle me.

Using a black marker, Yogi Bear draws a line on each bill and rubs the marked area with his thumb. Eventually, he hands over a huge bundle of worn out gourde notes and lets me count. It takes forever, as there are at least two hundred notes.

Half an hour later I'm on the veranda in front of my room with Kimmy, a photographer from Miami. We are surrounded by tropical vegetation and get a glimpse of the sea in the distance. Swaying in a rocking chair, I kick back a glass of Scotch, and slowly, the tension in my head eases.

Veranda with rocking chairs

The Oloffson hotel — once a stately private residence with the charm of a bygone era — is perched on a hill. It was built at the end of the 19th century and still retains the same look. They just freshened up the paint a bit.

Kimmy sips her drink and takes a deep breath. She photographed the riots and is exhausted. She works freelance for the *Miami Herald* and ended up at the Oloffson because she had read about the hotel's storied past.

"The place is magical," Kimmy says, "You can feel the people who have lived and worked here, it's more than a hotel."

She's right. Kimmy, for instance, is staying in the Graham Greene room, and I'm in the Mick Jagger room.

Kimmy wears a white men's shirt and military slacks with side pockets. I feel a connection to her. She's a freelancer just like me and knows the ropes. I wonder if I should ask her for a contact at the *Miami Herald*. Who knows, maybe I could land a story there one of these days.

I hold up my glass and give her a smile: "Cheers."

"Let's get this out of the way," Kimmy says. "I like women, okay?"

"Okay."

I finish my scotch and head to my room. There's a picture of Mick Jagger above the bed. He's sitting on the veranda in a rocking chair. Just like me a few minutes ago.

I examine my bed. Could this be the bed that Jagger slept in? Possibly. The frame is of solid wood which almost lasts forever. The only thing they probably changed is the mattress, although I'm not so sure. It seems to be very old and is worn out in the middle. Theoretically, it could still be the same on which Mick had his way with Bianca.

I'm heading to the pool and order a drink at the bar. The sound system is playing "Haiti, Cherie" by Harry Belafonte.

At the head of the pool, there's a large stone fish. Water gushes from his mouth into the pool. The Hotel Oloffson is famous because Graham Greene wrote his spy thriller *The Comedians* here. In one scene, a dead man floats in the pool.

Pool at Hotel Oloffson

The Comedians were made into a movie with Richard Burton and Elizabeth Taylor which resulted in international fame for the hotel. Like many other celebrities, Mick Jagger stopped by in the late sixties and gave a spontaneous musical interlude poolside.

"Another drink?"

I nod and the barmaid pours me another Scotch. I made friends with Kerline because she works at the pool bar, my favorite spot. She's twenty-eight and has an eight-year-old son. Shortly before the child was born, the father disappeared which is quite common in Haiti.

Kerline slides a napkin over the counter. She scribbled a few sentences in bumpy English. She writes that she is a member of a dance troupe, likes going to the movies and takes English classes. She shows me a photo of a girlfriend who married an American and now lives in Texas.

Haiti has a tumultuous history. Together with the Dominican Republic, it sits on the Caribbean island of Hispaniola. Discovered by Columbus, it became the first European settlement in the Americas.

Initially, the entire island was a Spanish colony, but in 1625, one third was taken over by the French. They brought in African slaves and cultivated coffee and sugar cane which was very profitable. Slaves outnumbered the French masters by ten to one, and in 1804 there was a successful revolt.

Power was taken over by light skinned descendants of French colonists and slave women who made up about ten percent of the population. And that's part of the problem even today: Power and money are in the hands of a corrupt few.

"Une bière, s'il vous plait," Kimmy says.

The photographer from Miami arrived at the pool bar. I am impressed. I had no idea that she speaks fluent French. Walking barefoot, she wears Bermuda shorts and a wife beater shirt.

Kerline gives her the beer and a glass. Kimmy shoves the glass aside, taking a good swig straight from the bottle. She jumps into the pool with a butt bomb, and the water splashes right up to the bar.

"She always gives me that look," Kerline whispers. "Somehow it makes me uncomfortable."

The hotel manager shows up. Richard is in his early forties and grew up in Connecticut, the son of a Haitian father and an American mother. He doubles as the lead singer of a rock band known throughout Haiti.

Richard is a bit stocky and his skin is almost white, his strongest African features being the dreadlocks spilling over his shoulders.

"Let me have a bottle of water", he says to Kerline. But then, he changes his mind. *"Ah, putain,* give me a glass of red."

Richard flips through a notepad until he reaches a page with my name. He gently touches my shoulder. "It's a bit embarrassing, but in the current situation we urgently need cash. Could I possibly collect the extras?"

Breakfast is included in the room rate, but I often had lunch and dinner at the hotel. And drinks at the pool, of course. Up to now, I simply charged it to my room number.

"How much?"

Richard shows me the total. The amount is a bit higher than expected, but it's difficult to trace, so I just pay him off.

"Thanks, man," Richard finishes his wine, pats my back and continues to Kimmy who's frolicking under the water jet of the stone fish.

In the evening.

Kerline's shift is over, and I join her to a live concert nearby. The stage is set up in a park. It's almost like a Roman auditorium. The audience sits on stone steps arranged in a half circle. Vendors are selling beer and meat skewers. I'm the only white guy and get the occasional curious look.

It's a concert organized by the opposition. A banner behind the stage demands free elections.

The band plays *twoubadou*, a music genre unique to Haiti. It's the Creole word for *troubadour* – a medieval poet who sings about love.

The name of the Band is *Ti-Coca*, Creole for "Small Coke." An odd name, but they seem to be a major act. The song is called "Twa Fey." No idea what it means, but the music is compelling. And they know how to play softly. The crowd of more than a thousand people keeps silent, listening in awe. Couples start dancing cheek to cheek.

Kerline gets up and sways to the rhythm. She takes my hand, pulling me up. After a while, I get the gist of it, and we're in sync. Kerline smiles. "Hey, you can dance!"

At once, there's an explosion.

People scream and start running. Some guys are throwing Molotov cocktails into the crowd. Probably secret police.

Kerline and I rush into a side street where it's completely dark. Almost all of Port-au-Prince is dark at night. There are only a few street lights near the presidential palace.

Kerline leads me back to the hotel. We hug spontaneously, and I can feel her heart beating.

"I know you won't come back," she says. "Nobody comes back. Because of this stupid violence."

She breaks away and disappears into the darkness.

At the hotel bar, I hear "Haiti, Cherie" again. Apparently, they're playing the same CD over and over.

4. A TURK IN NEW YORK – The world of Jimmy, the super

I'm in the boiler room with Jimmy. He's Turkish and a godsend, because he lends me fifty bucks. Jimmy's trust is partly based on my nationality. My credit score is pretty high with him, simply because I'm German.

For Jimmy, everything German means first and foremost: Reliability. Pretty amazing, considering the fact that Jimmy has never been to Germany and doesn't speak a word of the language. Nevertheless, he's a die-hard fan.

Without Jimmy I'd be in a pretty tight spot. Occasionally I get my journalist fees with a delay, and right now, I'm broke.

Jimmy and I kick back a beer in the boiler room. He wears a super's uniform: dark blue work trousers and a striped shirt in blue and white.

The boiler room is painted in industrial grey, including the floor and the ceiling. An interesting concept and quite efficient. You can paint the room in one go, without having to consider any straight lines.

A list of national holidays and the centerfold of a busty blonde are pinned to the wall, and above us, a maze of pipes stretch along the ceiling. Occasionally, there's a hissing sound, but Jimmy says, it's supposed to be this way.

Through friends, I have found accommodation in this commercial building. It's not approved for living, and except Jimmy, nobody knows that I sleep here.

I'm the unofficial security guard for the recording studio of a Jazz Rock band. The musicians are afraid that their expensive equipment might be stolen, and my rent payment to them reduces their own rent. It's a win-win, somehow.

Garment District in New York

Jimmy sips on his beer. "When I first heard about Germany, I was just a kid. Some of my relatives worked in Cologne, Berlin, Frankfurt. They brought back radios and electronic stuff. The Grundig shortwave radio was very much in demand as a gift. And then the cars. There were guys who went to Germany with nothing, and came back with a

Mercedes! It was a used one, sure, but they came back with a Mercedes!"

Jimmy's real name is not Jimmy, of course. His real name is Hayrun, but we are in New York and there's no time for complicated names. After a few futile attempts by his colleagues to remember the Turkish name, they christened him Jimmy. He doesn't really look like a Turk either, more like a Mongolian.

"My ancestors came from Turkestan, a region in China," Jimmy says. "They came to Turkey in 1948. I was born in Turkey, but I look Asian. Mostly people think I'm Chinese or something, but of course I'm Turkish. Absolutely one hundred percent Turkish."

We are drinking Beck's beer because Jimmy simply swears by everything German. He used to drink Heineken. Only recently he deciphered the small print on the bottle and found out that Heineken is from Holland. After that, he switched to Beck's.

"Two years ago, I was incredibly lucky," Jimmy says. "One day I walked around the Coney Island flea market and discovered a Grundig World Receiver. Even though the radio is about twenty-five years old, I knew it's top of the line. I check the back, and it says *Made in Germany*. I ask: How much? The guy says, forty dollars, the radio works fine. I say, forty dollars is too expensive, we're at a flea market, I give you five. At first, he says no, but when I leave, he calls me back: Okay, it's yours."

Grundig world receiver

The boiler room is Jimmy's castle. Here, he listens to music, reads the newspaper and occasionally guzzles a beer. Actually, he's not allowed to drink at work, but after 7 p.m., there's hardly anyone left in the building. Except me of course.

The fifteen-story building with its more than thirty companies produces a lot of jetsam, especially when someone moves out. Jimmy keeps the stuff with resale value and sells it off, making a few extra bucks on the side.

The building houses a marketing agency, two clothing manufacturers, a newspaper publisher, a photo studio and a company that produces chandeliers. And then, of course, there's the music studio in which I sleep as a security guard.

The building is a smaller version of the United Nations. Jimmy made it a sport to count the nationalities in the building and got to over thirty. There's even a Maori from New Zealand.

We take the freight elevator to the roof, using a special key. The building was constructed in the 1930s and resembles a castle. The fifteen floors taper off towards the top, and there are terraces on the higher floors.

On the roof garden, we have a panoramic view of Manhattan. The industrial buildings around us have weathered facades and are decorated with ornamental stucco. Some roofs even have spires.

On most floors there are offices or manufacturing facilities, but some lofts are obviously used for living which is not really legal.

In the seventies, the area around Penn Station was so dangerous that a lot of businesses moved away. To avoid vacancies, the real estate owners lowered the rent and leased to artists, turning a blind eye to the fact that most of them actually live there.

Jimmy points to a building on 28th Street where he spent his early days in New York. He manufactured motorcycle jackets with his brother Akif who came to the USA via green card lottery and eventually brought some family members over.

"The best sewing machines for leather are from Pfaff," Jimmy says. "Made in Germany, of course. The Pfaff 545 is amazing. Once you've worked with a 545, you don't want another one."

Jimmy says that Pfaff machines are the best, but also the most expensive. At some point, the Japanese developed machines that are almost as good but cost a third less.

Industrial Pfaff 545 sewing machine

"We couldn't believe it," Jimmy says. "Both machines are similar because the Japanese copied the design. But how did they manage to produce so much cheaper?"

Jimmy looks at me questioningly. I don't know the answer, of course.

"We opened the machines and looked inside," Jimmy says. "The Pfaff was shiny even on the inside and all parts were made of stainless steel. The Japanese machine was all raw inside."

Generalization is always tricky, but high-class engineering is definitely a German trait. Reliability is also a German trait, traditionally. But it seems to have been watered down lately. Graft, fraud and corruption are everywhere you look. Nowadays, Germany seems to be a country of crooks. But I won't tell Jimmy. Firstly, I don't want to ruin his illusion of an engineering paradise, and secondly, he might want to have his fifty bucks back.

I want to know why Jimmy no longer works in his brother's leather workshop.

"Basically, it's the same problem as with the Pfaff machines," he says. "The manufacturers in Asia offered similar jackets much cheaper. Ours were better, but at some point, the competition drove us out of business."

Manhattan Bridge

On a beautiful Saturday afternoon, Jimmy and I take the subway to Brooklyn. He wants to show me his home.

The Q-train rattles over the Manhattan Bridge and crosses the East River. A few ships pass underneath, and in the distance, we can see the Statue of Liberty.

Jimmy lives in a two-bedroom apartment in Sheepshead Bay, together with his wife, his daughters and his mother. It takes almost two hours to get there by subway.

When we step into Jimmy's living room, the Turkish top of the pops is running on TV. They receive it via satellite. Jimmy has built a surround sound system with old loudspeakers he scavenged from the trash.

There are three identical sofas, striped in red and gold, arranged in horse shoe fashion around the TV. I've never seen a living room with three sofas, but it looks cool, and Jimmy got them for little money at a closing sale.

While Jimmy disappears for a moment, his wife serves me a glass of tea. She is in her late thirties, but looks older. Maybe it's because she wears a headscarf. She gives me a smile but doesn't talk. She hardly speaks English.

Jimmy's mother joins us. She also wears a headscarf. One of her incisors is plated with gold, and she has the same Asian features as her son.

Jimmy comes back with his Grundig world receiver. Obviously, he has Turkish satellite TV now, but in his early days in America, the radio was his only link to home.

Jimmy kisses the device and holds it up. Even now, he uses it occasionally. When there's an important soccer match in Turkey, he takes the radio with him to work.

Jimmy's daughters come home. The elder is nineteen and a beauty.

"We want Shirin to get married," Jimmy says. "But she doesn't like anyone we introduce her to."

"What you want me to do, dad? Say I like them, when I don't?"

"We don't want to force her," Jimmy says. "And it doesn't have to be a Turk, but our tradition demands a Muslim."

"But a convert would do," Shirin says. "Wouldn't it?"

Jimmy sighs. "If need be, yes. As long as he's Muslim."

I want to know about the conversion.

"It's very easy," Shirin says and pulls a leaflet out of her bag.

The requirements are surprisingly simple. Actually, you just have to declare that there's no god but Allah and that Mohammed is his prophet. In Arabic. There's a phonetic transcription, and you just have to repeat it.

"Uh, if I were to say the sentence now, would I already be a Muslim?"

Shirin nods. Strangely enough, there's no mention about circumcision in the leaflet. I always thought, it's part of the deal. I keep the question to myself. Probably wouldn't fly in this family setting.

Jimmy puts the world receiver on a shelf. "Let's step out a bit. I want you to meet my friends."

We take the elevator and end up in the … boiler room!

Haki, the super, is also Turkish and has gradually brought more and more Turkish tenants into the building. Still, most of the residents are Russians. Sheepshead Bay, similar to the adjacent Brighton Beach, is dominated by Russians.

But the boiler room is firmly in Turkish hands. Or rather in pan-Turkish hands since the guys hail from all corners of the former Ottoman Empire: Romania, Bulgaria, Ukraine, Azerbaijan, Turkmenistan. Their connection is the Turkish language. Although different Turkish dialects are spoken in those countries, it's no problem to communicate.

"Our boiler room is sort of a Turkish clubhouse," Jimmy says. "A few garden chairs, a fridge and music, that's all we need."

At some point, the bleak concrete walls don't matter anymore, as the boisterous group recounts adventures from all over the world. Jimmy loves the cheerful atmosphere, especially since he can drink beer and *raki* here. At home, he never touches alcohol.

New guys are constantly coming in, bringing Turkish delicacies and drinks. Naturally, the boiler room is a purely male affair. It's unthinkable that one of the Turkish wives would show up here.

I tell them that I hail from Berlin and even picked up a few words of Turkish there. They are surprised that I'm familiar with the term *otuz-bir* which translates to "thirty-one" but also has a raunchy meaning. The guys can hardly believe that I know the bingo joke where the winning number is *otuz-bir* of all things, and I earn a barrage of laughter.

A Turkish hit comes up, and some of the guys are singing along. I'm a little drunk already. Beer and *raki*, *raki* and beer. A rather potent mixture.

Raki and beer

I remember Jimmy's daughter. "What's the deal with circumcision? A true Muslim must be circumcised, right?"

Jimmy nods.

"So not just the phrase ..."

Jimmy takes a sip of beer. "No. The *imam* will check you out. He wants proof that you're serious. You need to be circumcised."

"Does it hurt?"

"I was just a kid and I can hardly remember," Jimmy says. "But I know an adult convert who couldn't walk for two weeks..."

5. MAGNIFICENT MUMPIES – Being fat is beautiful: in Jamaica

"Well, I'm a skinny man," Charles says, "but I like fat women. I like them fleshy, strong, with a big bottom, you know? It really turns me on. A skinny woman has absolutely no chance with me."

Charles takes me through downtown Kingston in his minivan. He's forty-nine but could pass for thirty-five. A wiry guy with a sly smile. The whites of his eyes are brownish because he smokes a bit of *ganja* every few hours. He needs it to relax, he says.

I'm on the trail of a strange phenomenon. Contrary to the global trend, the Jamaican man loves it fleshy.

"We Jamaicans just respond well to fat women," Charles says. "Or at least a lot of us do. For instance, if we were to say: All those who like fat women on one side, all those who like skinny women on the other, there's no doubt that the majority would stand on the side for the fat ones."

The minivan hobbles over an uneven road. Kingston has seen better days. Some buildings have collapsed or burned to the ground. Small, ramshackle markets are scattered around town where vendors sell everything from bananas to car batteries. Some people walk barefoot.

"Look, a *Mumpy!*" Charles exclaims excitedly. He points to a bus stop, and his eyes start to shine. I don't understand what he means. A *Mumpy?* What is a *Mumpy?*

"Well, we have different names for the fat ones. Some call them Fatty, but most just say *Mumpy*. Some are very fat, but they look good. If they're well-proportioned, they'll appeal to a lot of men."

Most of the women at the bus stop are of normal size, but one has enormous proportions, especially the bottom. Is that a *Mumpy?*

Mumpy proportions

Charles nods enthusiastically. "Yeah, man! But that's nothing, wait till you see Melody."

We drive past Kingston Harbor, the seventh largest port in the world. It's the biggest hub for oil in the Caribbean.

The smell of beer hovers in the air. A Dutch brewery has a branch here. They brew, among other beers, the popular Jamaican brand *Red Stripe*.

Surrounded by the picturesque Blue Mountains, Kingston itself is to a large extent an ugly industrial city. The closest beach is almost two hours away. The capital has nothing of an island paradise.

Melody is not home, but we meet her cousin Tanesha instead. She is pretty and slender.

"Lots of Jamaican men like fat women," she says, "and sometimes when I walk down the street they yell, hey, skinny Minnie. That's their line. They say: You're just too skinny. Most Jamaicans want a fat, a very fat woman."

We settle down at a sidewalk café and wait for Melody. Charles wants me to meet her. The café is a hole in the wall with some plastic chairs in front. A rusty fridge hums behind the worn-out counter.

The owner has a black eye. Probably some domestic dispute. She is sturdy with a protruding bust. Charles hugs her passionately. Even though he works as a cab driver, he kicks back a Red Stripe and lights a joint.

"My mom, she's short and fat," Tanesha says. "And she has big breasts. My sister is fat, too. They take chicken pills which make your breasts and your booty bigger."

Tanesha tried to gain weight, too. She ate burgers and fries, but didn't gain an ounce. She also tried chicken pills, but her body doesn't tolerate the hormones. She gets headaches and diarrhea.

Chicken pills are used to fatten poultry and sold in animal feed stores for two US dollars a dozen. They contain hormones which can lead to breast cancer.

Tanesha says there's been a shortage lately. The chicken pills were sold out all over Kingston, and the stores started to require proof that the buyers actually have a chicken farm – which led many women to keep chickens at home, so they can officially register as chicken farmers.

Melody returns from a shopping trip, carrying two bags. She is dressed in tight, white jeans and a tight white T-shirt. Melody is enormous: about 400 pounds at a height of maybe five foot four. She has a rich boyfriend who, although married, can afford to support her on the side.

Charles gives her a tender kiss on the cheek. "She's not only a *Mumpy*, she's also a *Brownie*, a *Mumpy-Brownie*, so to speak."

A *Brownie?* In the US, it's a chocolate cookie of course, but what is a *Brownie* in Jamaica?

"A *Brownie* is a woman with light skin," Melody says. "When your skin color is not black, but rather light."

"The creams are called Mercury or Lexus," Tanesha adds. "We mix them together, pour them into a glass and apply the mixture twice a day. It gives you a nice color. It takes about a week, and it looks very good."

"But it doesn't work in the sun," Melody says. "You have to stay in the shade."

"I feel good when I bleach," says Tanesha. "My skin turns light brown, almost white. It looks very good, you know. The guys love it. It's just a beautiful color."

The creams are not exactly cheap by Jamaican standards. That's why many women focus only on the face. Some don't have the money to buy the expensive creams and use a homemade mixture of curry powder, toothpaste and toilet cleaner.

Homemade bleaching powder

"One guy even made a song about it," Melody says. She sings it to me: *Them-a-bleach, them-a-bleach for favor browning...*

Tanesha shows me the photo on her ID card.

Before the bleaching. "Look how ugly I was," she says. The photo was taken a year ago: Tanesha with flawless brown skin. A real beauty. Now, her skin is spotty beige.

Thursday night.

Ladies Night at the Asylum, Kingston's most popular nightclub. Admission is free for women, and there's a long line at the door. Two security guards and a Mumpy search the patrons for weapons.

Kingston is a tough place, and just a few days ago twelve people died in a shoot-out. It involved street vendors. The police wanted to drive them away from a lucrative location because they didn't have licenses.

The Asylum is packed to the brim. The DJ is a star in the Jamaican dance hall scene. Two camera crews walk around the place, filming the DJ and a few scantily clad Mumpies in blond wigs.

Melody and Tanesha took me to the club. Melody's sugar daddy has family obligations, and Tanesha is on the hunt for a boyfriend.

Fat Melody is greedily stared at by male eyes, but no one shows much interest in Tanesha. A guy buys Melody a drink and starts to chat her up, but a moment later, she leaves him standing at the bar.

Melody wears a weird outfit: Skin-tight jeans cut off at the hip, showing the upper half of her enormous bottom and a tiny G-string. In addition, she wrapped a flashing chain of lights around her hips.

Nightclub scene in Kingston

I am the only white person here and attract an occasional curious glance. Two young Chinese guys hang out at the bar. They seem a bit lost in the black crowd. There's a considerable Chinese minority in Jamaica. Most of them are ancestors of immigrants that came in the 1920s with the British.

"Buy me a drink, handsome?" One of the platinum blond Mumpies comes up to me. She wears a skimpy bikini and platform shoes.

"Sure, why not."

She orders a cocktail called *Alyssé*, which is popular with Jamaican ladies. It's a mixture of fruit juice and cognac and a bit expensive.

The Mumpy snuggles up to me. "Thanks, baby. — Really like your blue eyes!"

The lady thinks she's insanely attractive because most men here are lusting after her opulent forms, but I respond better to the slender type.

I notice that Tanesha looks at us. If she only knew that I like her much better than the Mumpies. Only her blotchy skin turns me off. She would look so much better without the bleaching.

The next afternoon.

I meet Tanesha at her workplace: Kentucky Fried Chicken. She wears the KFC uniform and brings me a *Smoky Mountain Barbeque Chicken* and a coke.

American fast food joints dominate the picture in Kingston. For each Jamaican restaurant there are at least ten American fast food franchises.

Jamaica's TV is almost completely American. The island sits in the same time zone as the east coast of the USA. As an American, you can go on vacation here without missing a single episode of your beloved sitcom.

Tanesha has been working at KFC for over a year, and eats the fast-food fare almost daily. Amazingly, she doesn't gain an ounce.

"Tomorrow, there's an outdoor bash in the park," Taneesha says. "Are you coming?"

The next day.

Charles, Tanesha and I are at the outdoor bash. A DJ plays records on an open-air stage, and the audience dances in a large, shallow pool filled with foam that sits in front of a huge slide.

Tanesha and I climb up the ladder and ride down the slide. With a splash, we land in the foam pool. People laugh and scream. Scores of couples dance in the shallow water, as a huge hose constantly pumps in fresh foam. It's the latest trend and called *Mud Slide.* No idea what this has to do with mud, but it doesn't really matter, I guess.

Dancing couple at the foam party

Most couples put on a hell of a show. They rub against each other, and it's almost pornographic. But that's completely normal in Jamaica. It doesn't mean, though, that after dancing, it will continue. Some couples put on a seemingly pornographic show and later separate without a word because they don't know each other at all.

Tanesha and I dance close together in the foam, and I try to do the same explicit mating moves as the Jamaicans. When in Jamaica, do as the Jamaicans do! I don't know if I got it right, but at least I try.

The foam gradually drenches our clothes, and the

Mud Slide takes on the quality of a wet T-shirt contest. Tanesha looks deep into my eyes, a look that means more than just dancing. "You know, some men like skinny girls. They think the skinny ones are easier to maneuver than a fat one." She laughs.

We knock the foam off our clothes and have a beer. We are both soaking wet, but it's actually pleasant in this tropical climate.

Charles is dancing with a Mumpy in the foam pool. He's right behind her enjoying her enormous girth.

A few days later.

Charles takes me to the airport. I gave Tanesha my address. She plans to visit the US since I told her that her type is in high demand there. Especially, if she would stop bleaching.

Charles swerves to the side to avoid a pothole. The roads are terrible in Jamaica.

"I'm waiting for my lucky break," Charles says. "I've been working for many years but nothing to show for. I don't have a house, I don't have a steady woman, and even the van doesn't belong to me. But I buy lottery tickets every day, and I don't think negatively. I feel that my dreams will come true one day, I just don't know when it will happen."

Charles hits the brakes. His eyes have that special glow again. Across the street, there's a Mumpy waiting at a lonely bus stop.

The bus drivers are on strike, so Charles hops out and offers a ride. The luscious lady wears a skimpy, red dress, a red cowboy hat and red cowboy boots with fringes.

Charles manages to make her laugh. I can't understand a word he's saying. Anyone who thinks English is spoken in Jamaica is surely mistaken. In Jamaica, English is understood, but not necessarily spoken. Jamaicans talk to each other in *Patois* – a sort of slang English with its own syntax and African loanwords.

The Cowboy lady gets into the van. Her name is Vicky, and she actually wants to go downtown, but Charles convinced her to come with us to the airport for a short while. After that, he'll take her to her destination

At the entrance to the airport, Charles pats me on the back. "So long, my friend."

He takes a look at the Cowboy-Mumpy waiting in his van.

"And come back soon. I think you bring me good luck." He laughs.

6. THE LOBSTER TRAP – A festival of a different kind in Rockland, Maine

I'm jolted awake by loud clanking of metal and bump my head against the roof of my car. I see stars. Where am I?

Slowly, I remember: I'm in Rockland, Maine. Last night, I parked my rental car on the side strip of a dark road. Apparently, it's on the route of the Lobster Parade. A marching band is playing right next to me.

Marching band at the Lobster Festival

Two kids stare at me through the car window. I make a face, and they disappear.

Last night, I could neither find accommodation nor

proper parking, so I just stopped on a side strip. In the dark, it looked fine. It's a miracle that they haven't towed me. Maybe the guy with the tow truck plays in the marching band ...

I slept on the backseat in an uncomfortable position. My entire body hurts. It was insanely hot in the car, and I'm in my undies.

I squeeze through the gap between seats and bump my head again. My rental car is tiny. I took the most economical option of course. In hindsight, I should have invested in a more comfortable model. But how could I know that the town would be filled to the brim during the festival?

I remember taking the key to the backseat and squeeze through the gap again. I fish the key out of the crack and squeeze through to the front. If I do this more often, I could probably follow in the footsteps of the great Houdini.

Driving slowly along the side strip, I manage to make a right turn into a narrow street. It leads me to a dirt road next to a forest. It's far enough from the hustle and bustle, and I park the car. Now, I urgently need a coffee!

After walking around town for twenty minutes, I end up in the waiting area of the ferry terminal. All coffee shops are packed, and people are waiting in line for a table.

My best option is the coffee machine in the ferry

terminal. It accepts quarters or single dollar bills, but I only have a twenty.

A middle-aged lady can make change. Nancy is waiting for the ferry with her nephew who lives on one of the islands. She wears a lobster hat.

Lobster hat

I feed the coffee machine with a dollar bill and select *extra strong* and *with milk*. It's no real milk of course, but that's okay. As long as I get my dose of caffeine, I'm fine.

The vending machine with the snacks is almost empty. Salted pretzels and a Whoopie Pie are the only options.

I select the Whoopie Pie. Never had one of those. It's black with a white filling and looks a bit like an oversized Oreo. The list of the ingredients takes up the entire back of the package. I start reading, but then I stop. Sometimes it's best not to know what's inside. The coffee hits the spot, and the Whoopie Pie doesn't taste too bad, either. I immediately feel better.

The ferry terminal overlooks Rockland Harbor. Boats are sailing across the bay, as the sun glistens in the waves. I tell Nancy that I like her hat, and she shows me what you can do with it.

"The claws and feelers are moveable. And if you get a little buzzed, you can turn them in a way that it looks crazy. It's fun with the hat. After all, we are at the Lobster Festival."

I'm a lobster fan and always wanted to know where they come from. Almost ninety percent of the world's lobsters are harvested off the coast of Maine. Naturally, they are much cheaper here than anywhere else. That's why I rented the car and drove 450 miles from New York.

On my way to the festival grounds, I pass the parade again. A group of veterans drive motor go-carts in carefully choreographed figure-eights. They each wear a Turkish fez and have trouble fitting their legs into the tiny vehicles. They also make a hell of a noise. It's not entirely clear what the go-carts and the Turkish hats have to do with the Lobster Festival, but it looks cool, and that's all that matters.

They are followed by a group celebrating the star of the parade: Six people carry a huge lobster made of cardboard. Interestingly, the lobster-bearers are themselves dressed as lobsters.

People cheer as a beauty queen passes by, perched on the back bench of a sports car. She wears a crown and a glittering dress with gloves reaching up to her elbows. Her sash reads: *Miss Lobster Festival.*

Festival tents in Rockland

The festival ground is packed. Apart from food tents, there are carnival attractions: Bumper cars, shooting ranges, a merry-go-round, and a nasty clown, sitting on a ledge above a swimming pool. He makes faces and insults people in the crowd. If you hit a target with a ball, the ledge retracts and the clown crashes into the pool. I've seen this in movies, but I didn't know it still existed.

SPLASH!

A young man hit the target and managed to sink the clown. The poor wretch, now soaking wet, climbs back on his ledge. He starts insulting the crowd again. It's a simple concept but seems to work. People keep buying the balls like crazy because they want to sink the nasty clown.

I wonder if the clown is his own boss. How much

might he make per month? Probably more than a freelance journalist. Considering the crowd buying the balls, he should have his pockets lined with cash at the end of the day.

It's not a bad idea. Why not try my luck as a nasty clown? All I would need is a portable pool, a target mechanism and a clown costume...

On second thought: It's probably not as easy as it looks. No business is as easy as it looks.

Firstly: It's a seasonal thing, and you have to be where the carnivals are. Which means, you need to deal with the carnival administration.

Secondly: You must have a certain talent to be nasty. You need to insult people enough to make them buy the balls, but you can't overdo it. There might be some guys in the crowd who don't give a rat's ass about buying the balls and just beat you up.

Anyway: It's a compellingly simple business model. I write a reminder on the first page of my notepad: *If all else fails, consider the clown!*

The huge lobster tent is equipped with long folding tables and benches. Basically, it's the same set-up as in a beer tent. The place is packed with people munching on lobster, and there's a long line. Self-service. Eventually, it's my turn.

"Single, double or triple?"

"Triple."

I receive a tray with three steaming lobsters for

twenty-nine bucks. Unbeatable. In New York this would cost a small fortune.

Triple lobster

The meal comes with a plastic bib, a bowl of melted butter, a corn on the cob and a bag of *Maine Coast* potato chips. The tray is made of recycled cardboard. Not very appealing, but what the heck. Lobster is lobster. I put on the bib and go for it.

The shell of my lobster is surprisingly easy to crack. It's about as thick as the shell of a peanut, and I don't need tongs. I remember it differently from restaurants. The shells were always difficult to crack.

The guy next to me says that these are *molters* because they just dropped their old shell. The lobsters do it every year so they can get bigger.

A glass of white wine would go well with the lobster, but there's a no-alcohol-policy. My neighbor points to a restaurant right outside the festival grounds. "You can get some there."

After my lobster meal, I head over to the restaurant. It's called "Conti's" and looks like a stranded ship inside. Fishing nets hang from the ceiling, old navigation instruments are on a shelf, and the lighting consists of candles and storm lamps. There's not a single electric lamp, and the tablecloths are old newspapers.

I run into Nancy again. In the meantime, she met her little nephew who's also wearing a lobster hat. Nancy works as a waitress here, but today is her day off. She's at Conti's, because she wanted to have a beer.

"The cook is also the owner," Nancy says. "John Conti. He does it all on his own in the kitchen. No one must go near his creations, or he will shoot you." She laughs and the feelers on her lobster hat wiggle a bit.

Nancy has lived in Rockland for thirty years. Does she know anybody who could take me out to sea sometime? I'd like to know how you catch lobsters.

"My ex is a lobster fisherman. He's a little difficult, but I can ask him, okay?"

I order a glass of Chardonnay. The waitress is a niece of Nancy's, and she also wears a lobster hat. Julie is pretty. She braided her hair to pigtails, and even the lobster hat looks good on her.

When Nancy mentions that I am a journalist, Julie shows me some photos of student theater performances: Julie as a witch, as a nurse in the

American Civil War and as a prostitute in lingerie, smoking a cigarette. She says that she can sing and considers a stage career.

"I know a musician who plays in the orchestra pit on Broadway."

"Really?" Julie wants my phone number. "When I come to New York, I'll call you."

A steel band starts playing on the pier next to the restaurant. The Caribbean sound and the ocean view are relaxing. It almost feels as if we were in Trinidad. But there's not a single black person in the steel band. Immigrants from the Caribbean are rare here.

Julie wants to know why I'm not wearing a lobster hat. She's got them for sale. Ten bucks a pop. I buy one and check in the mirror. Looks a bit stupid but so what? You gotta go with the flow.

I remember my rental car. Julie tells me that it's not allowed to park on that forest road. Shoot. Towing would be a costly affair, so I better move the car.

When I arrive at the dirt road, there's a police car with flashing lights. The officer was just about to write me up. He asks for my papers.

I produce my German license. Since I rarely drive, I still have the old grey driving license. It's not even a plastic card, it's a leathery booklet with a photo stapled inside. I never bothered to exchange it for a new card since the booklets have no expiry date. I don't think the Maine State Trooper has ever seen one of those. "What's this?"

I produce the certified translation from the German consulate, which says that the license is valid in the US. The trooper skims over the document and gives me a skeptical look.

"You're German, driving a car with Florida plates and are parked on a forest road in Maine?"

"It's a rental."

I fumble the contract out of my pocket, which states my New York address.

"New York, huh?"

The trooper's impressive hat is adorned with a gilded coat of arms, and the hatband ends in two metal pins. It seems that he's not particularly fond of people from New York, and I fear for the worst.

"You're here for the Lobster Festival?"

I nod, and the feelers on my lobster hat wiggle a bit. I had completely forgotten that I'm still wearing the hat. The trooper smirks.

"I like your hat, so I'll turn a blind eye today. But get off this road. I almost had you towed."

The next morning, six o'clock.

It's a beautiful day, and I'm on a boat with Nancy's ex-boyfriend Richard. I didn't sleep too well in that tiny car, but at least, I found a decent parking space.

Richard is about sixty-five and the quiet type. He wears dungarees and rubber boots. His scruffy hair is tucked under an old baseball cap.

The lobster boat is thirty feet long and powered by a noisy diesel engine. A sticker on the cabin reads: *Stop the talkin' and do the walkin'!*

Richard is at the steering wheel and looks annoyed. Troy, his young assistant, is a bit more talkative. "Lobsters are caught with the stinkiest, most rotten fish you can imagine," he says. "We use fish scraps that no one would eat, not even the other fish. But the lobsters are crazy about that rotten fish, and they crawl into the trap."

He shows me a bucket with fish scraps. The stench is repulsive. "When you eat lobster, you must always remember what they're feeding on. So, basically, that's what you eat."

Troy is thirty-five and has his hair tied back in a ponytail. In his spare time, he plays guitar in a heavy metal band.

We keep going further out to sea. A lot of buoys are floating around. Every few hundred yards, their color changes, indicating that the attached traps belong to a different fisherman. There are more than two million traps off the coast of Maine.

"Maine is remote," Troy says. "Nobody has to travel through. It's not on the way to anywhere, not even Canada. It's the only state with a single border – New Hampshire. Maine survives on tourism, on people like you who like lobster. At least in summer."

Okay, and in winter?

"In winter, all the tourists leave, and we're all alone. As for us lobster fishermen: It's damn cold here in winter, so we only fish from March to November. Then we sell Christmas trees, and we can do that until the end of December. After that, we disappear for two months. We sit at home by the stove and wait for spring."

Lobster boat with lobster trap

We've reached Richard's fishing grounds, and he stops the engine. His buoys are old detergent containers — the regular kind cost twenty bucks a piece.

Troy hoists up a lobster trap with a winch. The bottom is weighed down with concrete so it sinks better. Some lobsters of different sizes crawl around in the trap. Troy throws the big ones right back into the sea. Those are mating males, crucial for the preservation of the species. Some are pregnant females with dark red rye on their bellies. Those also go back into the sea. The rest of the catch ends up in a basket.

The traps are quite ingenious. The entrance leads to a conical net. When the lobster arrives in the *saloon* with the bait, it can't get out any more because of the conical form of the entrance. Unless it's a baby lobster and small enough to crawl out of a tiny exit hole.

But who's checking whether someone keeps the big males and the roe-bearing females?
"There's a coast guard," Troy says. "They're coming up out of nowhere with their speedboats, and if they catch you with a lobster that's too big or too small, you lose your license."

Two hours later we deliver the lobsters to the festival. They go into the *Biggest Lobster Cooker in the World.*

Lobster cooker

When the creatures are being lowered into the cooker, I perceive loud hissing which sounds like choked screams. Do lobsters feel pain?

"No, they are very primitive animals, like a worm or a spider," Troy says. "They have no central nervous system and feel no pain."

Lobsters have no vocal cords and cannot make any noise. The hissing comes from the air that escapes from the heated shells.

The last day of the festival.

It's a bit quieter since many people left already. I go for the triple lobster again. It's delicious, but I remember what Troy told me: Always consider what they feed on! I ignore the thought. The lobster meat is delicious, and that's all that counts.

Julie comes up to me, the aspiring actress. She asks when I will drive back to New York. Could she stay with me for a few days?

I confess that I'm living in a very small room that's even a bit tight for one person. Julie laughs and says it was just a joke.

After another night on the back seat of the car, I head home. When I turn onto the road that leads out of town, there's Julie on the side strip, carrying a a backpack. She motions me to stop.

I roll down the window, and she gives me an angry look, pointing at my license plate. "You're a liar, you're from Florida!"

"I'm not! It's a rental."

I show her the rental agreement, and she nods. "Ah, okay."

Julie says she has a friend who's a student at NYU, and that she can crash with her for a while. She just needs someone to give her a ride.

I tell her to hop in and step on the gas.

7. IN THE REALM OF THE ROOSTER –
Unexpected encounters in Puerto Rico

It's five o'clock in the morning, just before sunrise. The rooster opera has begun and will continue for hours. One of the birds seems to have a psychological problem: he keeps on crowing until two in the afternoon. Maybe he's a youngster and still practicing. His crowing sounds hoarse and sometimes breaks off.

Holiday resort in Rincón, Puerto Rico

I'm in Puerto Rico. Not in San Juan, the capital, but on the other side of the island, in Aguadilla. Or more precisely in a small hamlet called *Rincón* which means *nook* in Spanish.

In the photos, it looked great: a small studio with a view of the ocean for sixty dollars a day. The visuals are fantastic, but the acoustics are not. Because of the stupid roosters, I don't get my usual share of sleep and constantly feel tired.

Nine o'clock.

I'm on my way to the hamlet of Rincón. It's a fifteen-minute walk from my apartment. The road is lined with mango trees, and horses are grazing on a meadow. Some mangos have fallen down, giving off an intense smell. They are smaller than the ones I know from the supermarket – about twice the size of a plum. I wonder why nobody picks them up. Probably, there's just too many. I'll pick some up on my way back.

Rincón consists of one intersection and a few side streets. There's a supermarket, a pharmacy, two bars and an auto repair shop, and that's it. In the resort, a guy told me that if you drive through and blink, you might miss it entirely.

Stepping into the pharmacy, I can't remember the Spanish word for earplugs. I try it in English, but the lady behind the counter doesn't understand. I stick my index fingers in my ears: *" Protección para los oídos."*
"Ah, tapones!"
"Sí, sí, tapones!"
The lady doesn't have any. It's rare that someone

asks for them. She recommends trying at the shopping mall in Mayagüez about ten miles away.

Back in the resort, I'm in luck. Carmen and Vivien, who stay in the apartment next to me, are heading to Mayagüez with their rental car and offer to give me a ride. Both are Puerto Ricans who live in New York. They bought their apartment to relax here from time to time.

The shopping complex in Mayagüez looks almost like the one on Route 17 in New Jersey. The usual department stores are grouped around a huge parking lot: JCPenney, Kmart, Marshall's ...

Carmen and Vivien shop at Kmart, and I head to the pharmacy. They carry foam plugs, similar to the ones you get on a plane. Those hardly help at all and constantly fall out of my ears.

I ask for wax earplugs, but they're sold out. When will they be back? I get a shrug. Very rarely, somebody asks for them.

I buy some cotton balls and candles. Maybe I can manufacture my own earplugs. After all, the good ones are made of exactly those materials: cotton and wax.

An hour later.

We're back at the resort and play volleyball on the beach. Or rather, we simply try to keep the ball in the air since there's no net. Carmen and Vivien are in their early 50s but look younger. Both have enormous busts. Carmen has a light complexion and wears her black hair short. Vivien is well tanned and sports a dyed, blond ponytail. Both are single and have adult children in New York. They grew up in the US and speak better English than Spanish.

I notice envious glances from some Puerto Rican family dads, sitting on the terrace with their wives and children. Most of the apartments in the resort belong to wealthy families from Ponce or San Juan who spend their leisure time here.

Exhausted from hopping around in the sand, we settle down in the deck chairs on the terrace. There's a small bar run by the super and his wife, and it's time for a *piña colada,* Puerto Rico's national drink: a cocktail made of rum, coconut cream and pineapple.

Piña colada

On the way to the bathroom I run into Luis, the

super. He pats my shoulder. "You lucky son of a gun!"

I don't understand what he means.

"Well, before I was married, I also had a *ménage à trois*. Great stuff. All the guys envy you."

In the bathroom, I check my reflection in the mirror. *Lucky son of a gun!* So they think I'm having a *ménage à trois* with Carmen and Vivien. Actually, an interesting idea.

Back on the terrace, sitting smack in the middle between the two ladies, I can feel the envious glances of the family dads again.

A bit later, Carmen, Vivien and I drive to an open-air bar, which is perched high upon a hill. It has a fantastic sea view and is the best place to enjoy the sunset.

There's live music. I would have expected salsa or merengue, but the band is completely made up of Americans. Most of their repertoire are Santana covers.

Puerto Rico somehow belongs to the US, but somehow it doesn't. It's called a "free associated state." Puerto Rico has the dollar as currency, and besides Spanish, English is an official language. Puerto Ricans can't vote in national US elections, but if they move to the mainland, they can. They are allowed to work in the US, but in the Olympics, Puerto Rico has its own team. All this is kind of odd, and they had two referenda whether Puerto Rico should become a full-fledged US state or a sovereign country. Both times, Puerto Ricans decided on *neither-nor* and kept the current status.

The band plays "Black Magic Woman." Always one of my favorites. The rhythm and the sound of the congas blend in with the tropical landscape.

We drink rum punch – rum mixed with fruit juice. It's the drink of the hour, easy to make and instantly mood enhancing. Plus, it's only two bucks. At once, I feel that there are no worries at all. Really amazing what a simple rum punch can do!

Most guests are buff American surfers in Bermuda shorts and mirrored sunglasses. There's a faint smell of marijuana in the air. The surfers giggle constantly which kind of enhances my own vibe: *No worries, man!*

I start singing along with the song. *I've got a Black Magic woman, got me so blind I can't see* ... Ah, it's just great. First, I dance with Vivien, then with Carmen. Shortly after, we're dancing together. We have our arms around each other and our sweaty faces are close. Maybe it's the rum punch or the anything goes mood of the surfers, but suddenly, the *ménage à trois* doesn't seem so far-fetched at all ...

A powerful drum interlude kicks in. We break away from each other, and I elegantly dance around Vivien and Carmen. I do a hip swing here, a lunge there. But in the heat of the moment, I stumble over the leg of a bar stool and almost fall on my face. Luckily, I can steady myself and pretend that the move was part of the performance.

Sunset in Rincón

Taking a break, we settle down at the bar and enjoy the sunset. Vivien looks at me over the edge of her glasses. I sense that she's a little drunk. "Do you think I should get a breast reduction?"

I'm surprised at her candor.

"They're too big," she explains. "They put strain on my spine."

I tell her that most men would probably consider it a crime.

Vivien smiles. "I've heard that before."

As she leaves for the bathroom, Carmen moves closer. "We've got some chicken curry in the fridge. If you're hungry, we could heat it up in the microwave later."

Cock-a-doodle-doo ..., cock-a-doodle-doo ...

It's half past four the next morning. I'm jolted awake by the roosters again. My hangover is almost unbearable, and at once, my worries are back. Basically, my entire life is worrisome.

To make matters worse, we didn't even have a *ménage à trois*. After munching the chicken curry, all three of us were dead-tired.

I swallow an aspirin and guzzle down a bottle of water. Using the cotton wool and a burning candle, I try to manufacture some earplugs by dripping hot wax on the wool. At once, it catches fire, and I drop it all on the floor. I splash some water on the burning wool and manage to extinguish the flames, but the stench is terrible.

As I open the door to the balcony to let in fresh air, the song of the roosters pierces my brain even more. Cringing, I slam the door shut again, slump onto bed and cover my ears with pillows.

The doorbell rings. It's 10 a.m.

I slept like a log due to complete exhaustion. It must be Luis, the super. Wrapping a towel around my hips, I hobble to the door. My hangover is still pretty bad.

"What's up, man, I think you wanted to come to the cockfight?"

I tell him that I need a coffee first. I turn on the coffee machine, gulp down another aspirin and peel one of the mangos I picked up the day before. I cut my finger and quench the blood with a paper towel.

"What's that stench? Did you burn something?"

I explain that I tried to make earplugs with wax and accidently set the wool on fire.

"Earplugs? What do you need earplugs for?"

"The damn roosters, man."

Luis shakes his head in disbelief. "You gringos and the roosters ... I don't even hear them."

As I'm sipping my coffee, Luis tells me that he has been to the US.

"I was in Chicago for two weeks. It's easier to find work over there. We have a crisis here right now. I noticed that some things are cheaper in Chicago, especially electronics, but the rent is much higher."

Luis pours himself a coffee. He takes two heaped spoons of sugar. "If I had found a great job in the two weeks I would have stayed in Chicago, but of course it doesn't happen that fast. Besides, I'm used to a tropical country, and I have a job. I'd rather stay here."

Luis and I are on our way to the cockfight. On the back seat of his battered car is a cage with his rooster. It smells of chicken coop. A sticker on the dashboard reads *Jesús te ama!* – Jesus loves you. Next to it is an image of Wile E. Coyote.

Luis smirks. "The guy from 6D saw you coming out of 6F at 1:30 last night."

"We just had some chicken curry. Nothing else."

Luis looks at me in disbelief.

He parks the car on a dirt road next to the cockfight arena – a large tent with wooden benches inside. It's muggy. Some ventilators run on high speed, but it doesn't help much. Sweat runs down my face. There's a fight in progress, and Luis and I start preparing his rooster who will be next.

"Can you secure him?" Luis puts the animal in my hands. The rooster is trembling, and I can feel his heart beating. Using adhesive tape, Luis attaches an artificial spur at the back of the rooster's ankle – his weapon.

"Usually one of the roosters dies, but not always," Luis says. "The fight lasts fifteen minutes. If one of the roosters dies or remains on the ground, the fight is over."

The ring has a diameter of about five yards. The referee speaks through a microphone, amplified by a distorted loudspeaker. Today there are about thirty men and a few boys here.

Even in this simple arena the winnings and losses can go up to several hundred dollars, Luis says, but in the top cockfight clubs in San Juan or Ponce, it's really big business. Some of the best roosters cost up to $10,000 and people win or lose thousands in one night.

Cockfight

The fight begins. A plexiglass box is lowered from the ceiling. It has a divider in the middle and an access hatch on each side. Luis puts his rooster into one half, and the opponent puts his into the other.

The referee jerks up the box, and the roosters stand face to face. Oddly enough, they don't move. They just stand there. The referee grabs a rubber chicken and jumps into the ring. He teases the roosters with the dummy until they start attacking it.

When he retracts the rubber chicken, the roosters start attacking each other. Occasionally they leap up to injure the opponent with their spurs. After just a few seconds, our rooster flees the scene and flutters over the barrier. Luis catches him and puts him back in the ring.

The fight is getting intense. The crowd cheers the roosters. *"Pica, pica!"* – Stab him, stab him!

Eventually, our rooster remains on the ground, exhausted. Luis tries to fire him up, but he doesn't move. A gong sounds. Our rooster lost, but he's still alive. Technical knockout.

I'm back at the resort. Vivien and Carmen are preparing a barbeque on the communal grill in the garden. The guy from 6D, a family man in his mid-sixties, is giving advice on the available spices. He has a bottle of beer in hand. When he sees me coming, he gives me a knowing smile and says in English: "Puerto Rico very beautiful, no?"

Carmen wears sunglasses, and Vivien presses an ice

pack against her forehead. They haven't quite processed the rum punch either. Carmen offers me a meat skewer, and I kick back a beer.

A warm summer rain starts pouring down. The residents of the resort grab their things and rush back to the house.

Vivien does the opposite. She takes her beer and runs screaming through the rain to the whirlpool. It's a bit elevated and has a sea view. Vivien is waving to Carmen and me, and we rush over.

It's pretty cool. We're together in the whirlpool, and I'm in the middle. Water jets massage our tired bodies, and from above, a warm rain pours down on us. In one spot the sun appears among the clouds, and there's even a rainbow.

Whirlpool

I notice that the guy from 6D is observing us from his window.

"There's a rumor going around," I say. "They all think, we're having a *ménage à trois*."

Vivien takes a sip of beer and moves closer. "We must feed this rumor at all cost."

Carmen also snuggles up, and I suddenly feel a bit like James Bond.

"Actually, it's paradise here," I say. "The only problem is the roosters in the morning."

Two days later I'm back in New York. The garbage truck is in front of the building, making an infernal noise. It's half past five in the morning.

I've moved to a small studio in East Harlem, also known as Spanish Harlem or *El Barrio*. It took me quite a while to find a place with affordable rent. The apartment is an old walk-up, and at night, the neighborhood feels a bit dodgy, but you can't have it all.

I take a peek out the window. The Puerto Rican super, who has lived in New York for thirty years, puts some huge garbage bags on the street for pick-up. His name is Jesús. Not an unusual name in Puerto Rico.

I tell him that I just got back from Aguadilla and that it was great, except for the dang roosters crowing in the morning.

"Hey," Jesús says. "It's always something else. Here it's the garbage truck."

Jesús is right. Every Monday and Thursday the garbage truck makes a deafening noise. And it takes almost half an hour to get out of earshot. That's why I always have earplugs by my bed. Unfortunately, I forgot to take them to Puerto Rico. But how could

I've known that I would end up in the realm of the rooster?

I pop in the earplugs, and the noise of the garbage truck fades. I still hear it very faintly, but it's distant enough to fall asleep again.

I dream of Vivien and Carmen and the whirlpool, of chicken curry and delicious piña colada. And best of all: In my dream I've brought earplugs!

8. POINT BARROW, ALASKA – At the northernmost point of the USA

"In spring we wait with our *umiak* at the edge of the ice," Banna says. "The hull of the boat is coated with animal skins, and it's extremely lightweight. We use paddles, because we have to be as quiet as possible."

Banna is twenty-seven and an Inupiat Eskimo. He has parted his shoulder-length hair in the middle and wears a bracelet made of walrus ivory.

Umiak

"Giving it our all, we manage about 150 yards a minute," Banna says. "If a whale appears in our vicinity, we can estimate roughly where he will come up again. If he emerges just a bit and takes a short breath, he will take another breath after fifty yards. Then we jump into the boat and try to catch him. But if he comes up high and takes a deep breath, then he'll dive. So we don't start paddling at all because we won't see him again until next year."

I'm in Barrow, Alaska. Population 4,000, sixty-five percent of them Eskimos. Mean annual temperature: twelve degrees Fahrenheit. In winter it's completely dark for two months, and in summer there's constant daylight for two months.

Barrow has the worst climate in the US, and San Diego – thousands of miles away – has the best.

"We had a great whaler named Malik," Banna says. "His specialty was to jump from the *umiak* on the back of the whale and finish him off with his harpoon. Unfortunately, we lost Malik last year. Not in the hunt but in the towing of the killed whale. Malik's boat was in tow with other boats to bring the whale to the coast. His boat capsized and we couldn't get him out of the water fast enough. He froze to death."

The Inupiat still hunt the whales with *umiaks* just like their ancestors who migrated from Asia 5,000 years ago. Reason: The whales are scared away by the sound of motor boats.

Most Eskimos are quiet types. Almost all of them

wear dark, sleek sunglasses and look pretty cool. Banna, on the other hand, is a chatty guy, coming up with a quip for almost anything. He's the official tourist guide of Barrow and knows everyone and everything here.

But there are hardly any tourists now. The only candidates for Banna's *Artic Tour* are Jeff, a bird lover from Massachusetts, and I. The tour is scheduled for the day after tomorrow. Banna only does it once a week.

We are in early June, the time when the sun never sets. Unfortunately, it's constantly cloudy, and up to now, I haven't seen the sun. For days and nights on end the sky is simply grey.

The view from my hotel room, advertised as *sea view,* is not really what you would expect. The "Top of the World Hotel" is a two-storied container-structure. From my room on the second floor, I see a gravel road. Occasionally an excavator drives by for no apparent reason. I never see them doing anything with it.

Behind that gravel road is the Arctic Ocean. It's almost the same shade of grey as the sky, and sometimes I can't tell where the ocean ends and the sky begins.

At the water's edge there is still a considerable amount of snow. For the Eskimos, this snow strip is a sort of highway, on which they zip by with their snowmobiles. And they do this day and night since there's no day and night anyway.

The TV in my room is tuned to the local radio station. It's called Eskimo Channel. Not really politically correct, or is it?

"In the past, the term Eskimo bothered us," Banna says. "It doesn't originate from our language. It's an expression of the native tribes that live further south and means: *The people who eat raw meat.* That's accurate because we eat raw whale and reindeer meat. Nowadays, the term doesn't bother us anymore, and we even call each other Eskimos. But we'd rather be called *Inupiat*, which means *people* in our language."

I head to the supermarket at the other end of town. Barrow has a few restaurants, but their prices are steep, so I need to skip a meal here and there and have a snack in my room instead.

It's officially summer here, but I wear a winter jacket. The temperature is only slightly above freezing.

On a dirt road, some Eskimo boys do tricks on BMX bikes, wearing t-shirts and shorts. Apparently, two degrees above freezing is tropical here.

There's a playground, but it's not exactly a blast: a slide, two swings and a plastic dinosaur that wobbles when you ride on it.

Barrow's architecture is bleak. Most of the small

wooden houses are dusty and grey. Scrap metal and trash is scattered around. There's not a single tree, not even a shrub. The vegetation consists exclusively of tundra grass.

In summer, the Arctic has absolutely nothing of the white wonderland that is commonly associated with the Eskimos. Right now, it looks more like a dirty junkyard.

Street in Barrow

Barrow extends over an area of about six by six miles. There are no roads to other places. The nearest Eskimo settlement can only be reached by plane. Theoretically, it's possible to travel by snowmobile, but it would take days.

All goods come by air freight or by ship. But the ship only docks twice a year.

On the open lots between the family homes, there are grave crosses or whale bone burial markers. The cemetery is full, so the dead are buried wherever there's room. The permafrost starts just below the surface, and the graves have to be chiseled out of the rock-hard ground. Most of the corpses are just as well preserved as when they died: frozen in perpetual ice.

Deceased millionaires come to mind who have their corpses frozen for a possible "reawakening" in the future. The bodies are kept in cold storage somewhere in California. It's a costly affair, and their estate has to pay for the upkeep.

Barrow would be the low-budget solution. Once your corpse is in the ground, you're basically rent free!

Burial site in Barrow

I reach the supermarket. The A&C Value Mart is huge, and everything is about twice as expensive as in New York. I opt for sesame bagels and yogurt. Suddenly, I feel a craving for liverwurst. Don't know why, really. Maybe it's the climate up here.

In the meat department I discover to my great surprise *Braunschweiger Leberwurst*, imported from Germany. Four ounces for $9.99. Quite steep.

How the heck did it get here?

I try to imagine the journey of the liverwurst.

Considering my own travel experience to Barrow, it must have been quite a ride.

It probably went like this: First, you need the liver from a cattle farm of course, and then it must be processed with spices and packaged somewhere in Braunschweig. From there, it probably went by truck to the seaport in Hamburg and was shipped to a distribution center in the US, maybe in New York. Then it went to Seattle. Almost all goods for Alaska go through Seattle. From there, the liverwurst was flown to Fairbanks and once again transferred to a smaller plane heading to Barrow. Distance traveled: about 7,000 miles.

And now I hold it in my hands in the A&C Value Mart. Considering all this, it's actually a steal. I put the liverwurst in my cart.

Twenty minutes later, I'm in Pepe's, a Mexican restaurant decorated with sombreros and paper donkeys. The patrons are surprisingly diverse: two men from Samoa, a Croatian guy and a Jamaican. Mariachi music is playing over the sound system.

The waitress comes from the Philippines. Lita is about sixty and has beautiful hands with perfectly manicured red fingernails. There are only men here and when she passes by, all eyes are on her. Barrow has a large surplus of men.

Fran, the owner of the place, is in Fairbanks right

now buying restaurant supplies. The restaurant is full of pictures of her. She moved to Barrow years ago from Oregon, and in the early days, she came up with all kinds of ideas to attract customers. At Christmas she became Santa Claus, for Easter she morphed into the Easter Bunny, and when things were particularly bad, she waited tables in a skimpy bikini.

Fran has become a legend and was even a guest on the *Late-Night Show* on national television. Next to the cash register there's a framed article of the *Wall Street Journal* with the title "Tacos on the Tundra."

Banna and Fran's son, Joe, sit at a table next to the counter. The options in Barrow are limited, and you keep running into each other. Joe is short and skinny. He wears a bushy, blond handlebar-mustache and reminds me a bit of Asterix.

I join them and order caribou tacos. Tastes like beef, but it's cheaper since it doesn't have to be flown in. A beer would go well with the tacos, but selling alcohol is prohibited in Barrow.

"When I came here twenty years ago, there was a bar and also a liquor store," Joe says. "But we just had too much trouble with alcohol."

Banna nods. "Alcoholism had become rampant. When I was a child, alcoholism was everywhere."

Joe twirls his Asterix mustache. "The worst thing is the darkness in winter. If you don't have a job, you sit around at home and start drinking. You gotta think of something to do, otherwise you go nuts. Lately, there's a lot of new people moving up here because of the oil. But they can't deal with the harsh winter. Sixty-five days of darkness, mean temperature twenty below. It's not for everyone."

"Usually five new families move here in summer," Banna says. "But during the winter, four of the five give up because they just can't take it: depression, insomnia, irritability. It's called seasonal confusion — so they quit. It's natural selection, so to speak. You really have to be a tough guy to live up here." He laughs.

Because of the alcohol problem, Barrow has a vote every October on whether the following year should be *dry* or *damp*. The last few years the town has been *dry*. Alcohol was illegal. But now it's *damp*: you can drink alcohol at home but are not allowed to sell it. You have to undergo a background check, and the city council determines how much alcohol you can buy. You have to place a collective order in Fairbanks and can only order once a month.

When I pay my bill, the waitress slips me a note: *Live on second floor. Have drinks for sale.*

Back at the Top of the World Hotel, I realize that the programming of the Eskimo Channel is a bit limited, featuring either traditional Eskimo music, the weather forecast or some old chestnuts like "Love Letters in the Sand."

They announce a dance party in the community hall for next Saturday. Each woman will receive a rose as a gift. A rather noble gesture, considering that the roses have to be flown in, but it will probably boost attendance.

I look out the window. Still the same cloudy sky, still the same gray. It's already past midnight, but it looks exactly the same as two in the afternoon. On the narrow snow strip at the shore, there's a lot of snowmobile traffic. The Eskimos have hitched trailers to the vehicles, transporting something. Are those parts of a hunted whale?

I remember my arrival at Barrow's small airport and the conversation with the taxi driver. At first, I thought the man with the dark sunglasses was an Eskimo. On the way to the hotel, however, he turned out to be a Filipino who's not particularly fond of Eskimos. "They're all alcoholics," he said. "And because of them, I have to pay a hundred dollars for a bottle of vodka."

I can't go to sleep. There's light coming through the sides of the curtains, and snowmobiles are zipping by every other minute.

I decide to take a walk. Maybe that'll get me sleepy. It's past 1 a.m., but the kid's playground is busy During the summer holidays, the parents let their children play for as long as they want. They have their own sense of time and return home when they get hungry.

The kids play Eskimo trampoline with a circular leather sheet that has handles at the edge. One little guy is on the sheet while the others hold the handles. On three, they pull the sheet straight which propels the little guy a few yards into the air.

Eskimo trampoline

Seems to be a lot of fun. They all laugh and cheer. Certainly beats the plastic dinosaur. The little guy actually closed his eyes while flying through the air. You will only do that if you trust that the others will catch you, of course.

It's an Eskimo tradition. Children learn at an early age that they need to rely on each other as a group. Only then can they survive the harsh conditions. This is important in whale hunting and in basically every aspect of their traditional lifestyle. A catch is always shared with the entire community, even with families who didn't take part in the hunt.

Town hall is a small, unimpressive building and quite dusty. A sign post gives the distance to several destinations: Los Angeles, Paris, Chicago. No matter which way you turn, from Barrow basically everything is thousands of miles away.

Sign post in Barrow

The Mexican restaurant is already closed, but on the second floor the lights are still on. I throw a small stone against the window. Shortly after, the waitress lets me in.

Up in her room, Lita unlocks a massive closet with liquor: bottom-shelf brands. I point to a bottle of whiskey. "How much for this one?"

"Two hundred."

I almost faint. The same bottle costs about thirty in New York.

I point to some vodka. "And this one?"

"One hundred."

Exactly the price the cab driver gave me. In New York, that brand costs about ten.

"Do you know the cab driver?" I ask.

"Sure, we're the only Filipinos here. But he's new and he doesn't have a liquor license."

Vodka actually lifts me up, and I would probably not go to sleep anytime soon. But a whiskey would do the trick. I search my wallet.

"Only have one fifty right now."

"It's okay. You can bring the rest tomorrow."

She hands me the whiskey.

"Shall we have a drink?"

Lita gives me a conspiratorial look. "Okay." She fetches two glasses, and we cheer. I get a buzz almost instantly. It feels like we are doing something forbidden which adds to the excitement.

Lita tells me that she worked as a nanny in California for a teacher couple with two kids. They received an attractive job offer from the school in Barrow, and she joined them. The teachers could not bear the conditions and left, but Lita stayed. Why?

"Sure, it's tough," she says. "But I make good money up here."

She shows me photos of her family in a poor district of Manila standing next to the appliances she financed: a fridge, a TV, a washing machine …

"Of course, I want to go back," she says. "But my family needs the money transfers. They are building a house for me over there. I must stay a little longer to make it all work."

We share another drink, and I glance at Lita's neatly manicured fingernails. The guys in the restaurant all stared at her hands. I imagine what she could do with those beautiful hands.

We are basically at the end of the world, but it's easy to forget. Lita has blacked out the daylight with some heavy curtains and lit some candles. We sit on a comfy couch kicking back Whiskey, and it almost feels like we are in an exclusive, private lounge bar. I glance at her hands again, and suddenly our eyes meet. Does she know what I'm thinking?

I put on a smile. "Real cozy place you got here ..."

"Yeah, I try my best to make it homey inside. I mean, look at the outside ..."

At once, she yawns. "Sorry, need to go to sleep, now. Until next time."

She gets up and tucks away the glasses.

I walk back to the hotel, carrying the rest of the whiskey hidden under my jacket. Well, at least I have my sleep medicine now. I will kick back one more shot, and that should do the trick.

Two days later.

The big day is here! New tourists came in by plane, and we have enough participants for the *Arctic Tour* with Banna's battered van. Apart from me and Jeff, the bird lover from Massachusetts, there's an older couple from Connecticut and Ryan, an African-American from Maryland.

Banna's van rumbles over gravel roads and leaves a cloud of dust behind. There's not much to see, but Banna proudly presents all institutions anyway: the fire station, the police office with a tiny jail, the church, the infirmary, the dentist, the chiropractor and even the dry cleaning. Those are landmarks here simply because they exist at all.

Banna is proud of the new school. The adjoining gymnasium even has a wall where you can practice mountain climbing. The tallest "mountain" in Barrow, however, is a pile of gravel about ten yards high. The school cost seventy-five million bucks. Every single stone arrived by ship and some items even had to be flown in.

Each resident of Barrow receives a grant from the state of Alaska. About $1,800 a year. The Eskimos get extra money from the Association of Native Americans. $5,000 a year per person.

If you marry an Eskimo woman and have several children with her, you can get up to $50,000 in support per year. The grants have something to do with the oil fields nearby. They are part of a deal for the mining rights.

Banna steers the van through the tundra. Jeff, the bird lover, mounts a camera with an impressive zoom lens, and Banna grabs his binoculars. It's all about spotting rare birds, the snowy owl for instance. Maybe we'll even see a polar bear or a walrus.

The tundra seems deserted. Not a birdie in sight, absolutely no sign of life.

Jeff tells me that this part of the fascination. It's precisely because the birds are so rare and manage to survive in this extreme environment that they are so interesting.

Banna stops the van and points to the right: "Look! Some arctic snipes."

In the distance I discover two small dots, hardly visible to the naked eye. Jeff zooms in and takes pictures as if it were a matter of life and death. "Wonderful..." he moans. "Ah, incredible..."

I borrow Banna's binoculars and look towards the birds. They are not much bigger than sparrows, and their plumage is not very exciting either: brown with a few white spots. They peck around for a while near a swampy spot and flutter away.

Banna moves on. His gaze wanders over the landscape, eager to discover a living creature.

"I've had several encounters with polar bears," Banna says. "Last October I was driving around town in my van, and when I parked, a polar bear peered into the window. My heart skipped a few beats. The bear can kill you in the blink of an eye. Last year we had over eighty of them in town. They were everywhere, and the police had their hands full keeping them away."

Polar bears are nomadic and unpredictable. They invade human settlements because they are hungry and can't find food anywhere else.

In Barrow there's a small museum with stuffed animals and traditional Eskimo tools. They also have an impressive specimen of a stuffed polar bear.

Stuffed polar bear in Barrow

"The Coca-Cola people came here to make a commercial," Banna says. "They went out on the ice to look for polar bears, but they couldn't find any. Then they heard about our museum. We took the stuffed bear down to the beach, and they filmed it. It's the bear in the original Coca-Cola commercial before they introduced the animated version."

We stop at an info sign in the middle of the tundra. No idea why they put it up here of all places, because otherwise, there is nothing to see far and wide. The sign shows the snowy owl that gave Barrow its Eskimo name: *The place where the snowy owl is hunted.*

Snowy owl

The owls weigh about two pounds and are said to taste like chicken. But hunting them has been banned because they are an endangered species.

Below the image of the owl there's a drawing of a traditional igloo. It's not made of snow but of clay.

Banna is debunking some Eskimo myths.

First: Eskimos have never lived in snow igloos. They only built them as emergency shelters when they were caught in the wild by a storm.

Second: Eskimos never rubbed their noses together as a kiss.

And third: No Eskimo ever offered his wife to a guest.

Banna spreads his arms. "Sorry, folks, it's all B.S.!"

I want to know why almost all Eskimo men wear sunglasses. Sure, it makes sense to shield the eyes from the intense glare when the sun reflects in the snow, and in fact, the Eskimos already fashioned protection goggles from bones thousands of years ago. But why do they wear them now when the sky is grey?

Goggles fashioned from bone

Banna smirks. "Well, there would be no need for them now, but the guys simply got used to them. And it looks cool, doesn't it?" He pulls me close. "It also nicely covers bloodshot eyes …"

We arrive at Point Barrow, a peninsula that juts into the arctic sea. It's the northernmost spot of the US.

As we get off the van, Banna points to the ocean. "Whales!" We grab our binoculars and indeed: In the distance some whales pass by and majestically blow up fountains. But in an instant, they submerge and don't come up again.

Banna looks at the crowd. "You hear that?"

We prick up our ears and give each other questioning looks. What does he mean? Banna savors the moment.

"Silence!" he whispers. "Arctic silence!"

He closes his eyes and we do the same. It's a magical moment. Absolute silence.

9. GO GREYHOUND – By bus from New York to Atlanta

J-55 is a fair-skinned African American with freckles, sitting next to me. He wears a baseball cap and baggy pants. The Ghetto Blaster on his lap has seen better days, and behind his ear is a half-smoked cigarette.

We are on the Greyhound bus from New York to Atlanta, and we both know we have a long night ahead of us. The bus is the cheapest way to get around, but it is also by far the toughest.

Greyhound bus

J-55 lives in Brooklyn, and it's not his real name of course, but in the hip-hop scene you need a catchy moniker for street credibility. He's trying his hand at songwriting and mixing and is on the hunt for a record deal. So far with moderate success.

Also travelling: an elderly lady with a sunken upper lip, wearing a wig, an aging rock musician with a tattered guitar case and a Mexican who's only piece of luggage is a bulging garbage bag.

I check the schedule. The stops on the way to Atlanta are as follows: Baltimore, Richmond, Greensboro, Louisville, Charlotte, Salem and Lynchburg. LYNCHBURG?? I take a closer look. No, I'm not mistaken. The town is called Lynchburg.

J-55 checks out two black girls who sit across the aisle a few rows ahead. He smirks and says that the arduous journey sometimes has its pleasant sides. What does he mean? Did he ever hook up?

"Yeah, sure, man," he says. "You meet women on the bus, of course. It's usually when you switch buses that you get closer. Somehow everyone is just passing through. You don't really want to meet anybody and you don't know what kind of problems people have in their lives. It's a bus love, a short stop, so to speak."

J-55 tells me a few erotic details of his adventures on the bus seats. Maybe he embellishes it a bit, but even if he exaggerates, I'm sure that a lot has happened on those buses, especially during the night.

It's 10:45 p.m. We're a couple of hours from New

York, and the bus makes its first stop in Pennsylvania. Most rest stops don't have names, but this one is named after Walt Whitman. It isn't exactly doing the poet justice. There's a fast food joint with extremely obese wait staff, a shop for travel supplies and a few vending machines with plastic toys.

"Can't wait to get to Atlanta," J-55 says. "The girls wear much shorter skirts over there, you know? If you play your cards right, you can get something cooking the first night. You just gotta sweet-talk a bit. It's a lot harder to get girls in New York. If you give them a friendly *hi* in New York, they just walk by like you're dirty or something. But in Atlanta, man..."

J-55 bites into a double cheeseburger he purchased at the fast food joint. Waiting in line for the burger, he tried to hook up with the girls from the bus, but it didn't work.

Midnight. We're somewhere in Maryland. Most of the passengers have dozed off, and it's quiet on the bus.

J-55 has turned to the side and pulled the baseball cap over his face. He snores. I am tired but can't go to sleep. The seats are uncomfortable. If I could just stretch out somewhere ...

Travel Plaza Baltimore. The bus station is next to a huge sports stadium. It's way past midnight now, and I still haven't slept a wink.

A few people get off, and two seats next to the bathroom become available. I rush over to claim them.

I try to find a way to get into a horizontal position. My upper body fits on the two seats, but my legs reach across the aisle to the opposite row of seats and block the access to the bathroom. So, what. Whoever needs to go, can simply step over my legs.

The bathroom door doesn't close properly, and is slightly agape. An unpleasant smell lingers in the air, but I fall asleep anyway.

A pothole catapults me back into the harsh Greyhound reality. The armrest is squeezing into my thigh. It hurts, and I groan. The Russian woman sitting in front of me wakes up and gives me a dirty look, as if I had touched her in a sexual way.

"What you do, you, you ...?" She stutters in broken English.

"Sorry, just trying to sleep, that's all."

Half past two in the morning. Richmond, Virginia. Our bus has an engine failure. We must wait in the station for the next one. Approximate arrival time: in two hours.

The bus station in Richmond is a mixture of homeless shelter and mental institution. Sitting opposite me is a man about fifty with a freshly sewn head wound and a hospital identification bracelet around his wrist. He looks like he just jumped off the operating table.

Next to the hospital guy is an aging punk rocker with a mohawk, a painted leather jacket and worn sneakers that seem two sizes too big. Apparently, no one told him that he's a few decades too late for punk rock. Or maybe, he just found his style and is reluctant to change.

A few homeless people spend their night here. They keep their belongings in shopping carts and have blankets and sleeping bags.

The travelers do not sit on benches but on their luggage directly at the platforms. Greyhound's got a *first come, first served* policy. If you are at the back of the line, you might not get on and have to wait for hours for the next bus.

J-55 sits on his backpack. He's crouched over on his knees and snores. Seems to be able to sleep anywhere, the lucky son of a gun.

I sit behind him on my bag and rest my face in my hands. But there's no way I can sleep in this position. It's noisy as hell, and there's always some nutcase screaming or talking to himself. Or two of them pick a fight. At five o'clock in the morning.

Our bus is called out, and the people in line come alive. There's a lot of pushing and shoving since the exact positions in the line are somewhat blurred. I can hardly believe it, but I am the last person to get a seat. The people behind me have to wait for two hours for the next bus.

Eight o'clock in the morning. We're driving

through Charlotte, North Carolina. A neat town with colonial-style houses.

We are having breakfast at a rest stop. I get scrambled eggs and baked potatoes from the buffet and wash it down with a large coffee.

J-55 kicks back a beer. "Coffee gives me heartburn," he says. He seems to be well rested and looks as good as new. Amazing.

A few hours later we reach Atlanta.

J-55 is picked up by some buddies in a convertible, and he jumps into the back seat with graceful leap. They'll be heading to a pool party. J-55 had offered me to join in, but I just need to get some sleep.

I discover a Super 8 motel. I've stayed in one of those before. Super 8 was founded in the early seventies, and a room cost $8.88 back then, hence the name. It's more expensive now, of course, but still one of the best deals.

The furniture in my room is a bit worn, but it's clean. The window leads to a dark backyard. I don't care. Actually, not too bad. It's probably quiet. I just need a shower now, and then I will delve into the sweet land of dreams.

The bathroom was installed later and is a bit elevated. Being dead tired, I stumble over a step and fall forward. I cut my finger on the sharp edge of the shower door. Blood drips onto the floor. I curse and stop the bleeding with toilet paper. To hell with the shower! I slump down on the bed and instantly fall asleep.

I wake up in the afternoon. The cut in my finger hurts, but it doesn't bleed anymore. I take a shower. and make sure that the injured finger doesn't get wet. I feel fine again. Atlanta, here I come!

To my surprise, the streets of downtown Atlanta are deserted. It's Saturday afternoon.

Downtown Atlanta on the weekend

Next to a subway station is a lonesome homeless man. I ask him what's going on.

"Downtown is business, man," he says. "Didn't you know that? Downtown is dead on weekends."

I decide to visit the birthplace of Martin Luther King. The memorial is closed for renovation. The area around Auburn Avenue seems deserted. The small houses are well kept and have manicured front lawns, but there's not a soul to be seen.

I can't find a restaurant. Just a fast food place with fried chicken. Not exactly my favorite dish, but I'm hungry. I nibble on a chicken thigh and drink a coke.

J-55 gave me his number, and I call him. In the background I hear party noises. "Sure, man," he says. "Come on over, it's off the hook!"

"Bankhead?" The cab driver looks at me in disbelief. "Are you sure you want to go to Bankhead?"

The driver explains that the area is a ghetto. I tell him to take me anyway. Half an hour later we arrive. The neighborhood has seen better days. Several dilapidated houses have barricaded windows, and seem to be abandoned.

There's trash on empty lots, and a patrol car with flashing lights sits at a street corner. The police officers wear protective gear.

Outside a liquor store some guys are drinking, their booze covered by paper bags. There are only men in the street, and they're all black.

We pass a row of public housing buildings. Black children run around on a playground, guarded by black women.

In a small park, I spot a group of young men. They sport hip-hop gear: baggy pants, baseball caps, gold chains. One of them has a gun tucked in his belt. There's not a single white person in sight.

The cab driver stops. "Here we are."

We're in front of a detached house with a large entrance gate and a massive wall, protecting the property. All window shutters are closed. Doesn't really look like a party. Besides, there's a rusty fridge dumped in the empty lot next to the house.

The driver looks at me with concern. "Are you sure you want to get off here? With your pale complexion, you're a walking target."

He has a point. I grab my cell phone and call J-55. Seconds later he comes out the door. "Welcome, man, good to see you!"

The interior of the house is neat and clean. Middle class. The party goes down in the garden which has at least 10,000 square feet. A DJ plays hip-hop. The girls sit by the pool, wearing bikinis. Meat sizzles on a barbecue grill, and it smells good.

Once again, I'm the only white person and sense that some of the guys are looking at me suspiciously. Do they think I'm a snitch?

Party in Bankhead

J-55 introduces me to the host: P.J. He's more than six feet tall and has a big grin on his face.

"My buddy here is a journalist from Europe," J-55 says. "We met on the bus."

P.J. pats my shoulder. "Welcome, man."

I start to feel better. Nobody gives me a funny look anymore.

"Is a community event," J-55 says and holds out a cigar box with money. "You contribute what you can."

I drop a twenty into the box.

J-55 chats with the girls at the pool. The guys at the party wear the same hip-hop gear as the ones I just saw in the park. Except, nobody has a gun. At least it's not visible.

One of the girls gives me the eye, but I better be careful. First, I need to figure out how the cookie crumbles around here.

The host hands me a plate with barbecue meat. "Atlanta's great, ain't it?" P.J. points at the bikini girls and the pool. "Small paradise, ain't it?"

I nod. It's really cool in the garden.

"T.I. and André 3000 are from Bankhead. Did you know that?"

I didn't. But I've certainly heard of them since they are famous by now.

"CNN, Coca-Cola and the Olympics. That's what

people connect with Atlanta," says P.J. "Why don't you write something about Bankhead?"

I tell him that I will.

"Okay," P.J. says. "What do you want to know?"
I congratulate him to his nice property and ask him how he got it. P.J. says he was born and raised here, and that he runs an auto repair shop.

"When people hear Bankhead, they always think drugs, but that's not true, my friend. There are some people who make their money honestly."

The bad image of the neighborhood has given him an advantage. He could afford the property because the real estate prices are moderate.

P.J. finishes his coke-whiskey and takes off his shirt. "Pretty warm today." He jumps into the pool. Right away, a couple of girls are by his side. P.J. is the man of the hour. I can see why Bankhead is paradise for him.

The girl who had given me the eye settles down next to me. "If you're a journalist, why don't you take pictures?"

"Not sure if taking photos is welcome here."

"Bullshit. You already know P.J., and he's the boss here."

The young lady starts posing. She positions her bikini booty right in front of me and looks over her shoulder. I take a picture with my cell phone. She gives me a few more poses, and I take a several pictures, including some with J-55 and other girls.

"Let me see." Keisha wants to see the photos.

The snapshots don't look too bad. A pretty girl in the sun always looks good.

"Wanna have some fun? P.J.'s got a guest room. Of course, it's not completely free."

I'm a bit surprised by the candid offer and tell her that I have a limited budget. I wonder if P.J. might be running a business other than the repair shop.

Keisha shows me her painted fingernails which are almost two inches long. "The beauty parlor costs, honey, and I need a little something for that, you understand?"

When she realizes that I'm not interested, she leaves.

J-55 approaches me. "Hey, man, Keisha is totally hot. Why don't you want to go to the room with her?"

"No money, man. Would I have taken the bus otherwise?"

J-55 smiles. "Yeah, sure. But that's exactly why I took the bus, so I've something left to contribute to the beauty expenses. If you don't want to go with her, I'll take her to the guest room, okay?"

Shortly after, both of them disappear in the house.

A few days later, I'm back in New York. I receive a message from J-55, asking me for the photos. Nobody shot decent photos that day, and he needs them to commemorate.

I send him the photos and ask what's there to commemorate. He replies that he's together with Keisha now and simply stayed in Atlanta. He found a job in a copy shop. Nothing fancy, but it's a start.

He writes that he thought about moving to Atlanta for a while already. It's simply warmer, and he doesn't just mean the temperature. At the end he adds:

And you know what's best about all of this ...? — No Greyhound anymore!!!

10. BE FUNNY! – Job search in Tokyo

"You need a tie, man," George says. "Didn't anybody tell you?"

George is from Nigeria and lives with me in a *Gai-Jin House* – a cheap guesthouse where most foreigners end up when they come to Tokyo. George is my tutor in Japanese etiquette. He's been here much longer and knows his way around. And he speaks surprisingly good Japanese. He's got linguistic talent.

George looks a bit like Mister Clean: He wears a golden earring and has a shaved head. He doesn't need a tie anymore since he has found a job as a DJ in an underground club in Shinjuku. There, he can wear whatever he wants. He lends me one of his old ties: "Good luck!"

The metro train glides almost silently over the tracks. I didn't get a seat and secure myself, grabbing a handle. My new teaching job is in Yokohama, the port of Tokyo. It's basically the same city but it takes about one hour by express train to get there.

Metro train in Tokyo

I have a panoramic view over the heads of my fellow passengers. Here, I am taller than average. Since the Japanese are all about the same height, their black hair forms an almost even surface. It's eerily quiet in the packed train. Nobody talks, and many passengers have their eyes closed.

The weather is cloudy, even a bit gloomy. Right and left, a concrete jungle of small houses stretches out. High-rises can be found only in certain areas. Tokyo is earthquake prone. Smaller houses are safer. It's extremely expensive to build skyscrapers that don't collapse when the earth trembles.

Between Tokyo and Yokohama there's hardly an open spot for miles and miles on end. It's rare to see a tree or some greenery. Tokyo is one of the most densely populated metro areas on earth. More than thirty million people live in a radius of twenty miles around the central station.

The train is plastered with advertising posters. It seems that they used every available square inch. As a sport, I try to decipher some of the characters. I once took a Japanese course and can communicate to some extent.

The train stops in Yokohama, and I hop off. It's drizzling. Small streets have no names in Japan. It's a strange system with numbered blocks, that's even hard to understand for Japanese. House numbers do exist, but they are not in consecutive order. They've been assigned according to when the property was registered with the housing department. Finding an address is insanely complicated. When you need to go somewhere new, you always receive some drawing with reference points. Otherwise you will never find it.

Japan is by far the best organized country I've ever been to, and it's an absolute mystery to me why they haven't changed this ancient numbering system.

On second thought: Japan has about 120 million people and probably countless millions of property records. Changing all this would have a ripple effect through the entire economy. Practically all official docs would need to be changed, including IDs and all records of utility companies, health care providers, insurances ... It could create chaos and even topple a government.

But that's not really my problem. My problem is that I have exactly two minutes to get to my appointment. Tardiness is not an option in Japan. Being late equals being fired.

The boss of the temp agency drew me a map. The tutoring school is only a few hundred yards from the train station.

I start running, but after a few steps I realize that I'm heading in the wrong direction. I make a U-turn and step into a puddle. Dirty water splashes on my pants. Shit.

But at least I'm heading in the right direction. I recognize the supermarket that's on the map and also the flower shop. The Japanese are staring at me as I run by. Foreigners are rare in the suburbs.

I arrive at the school one minute late and soaking wet. It's a private tutoring school, housed in a four-room apartment. Two small boys are running around in the hallway, and I remember what the boss of the agency told me: "Funny!" he said. "You must be funny! That's what's most important."

Funny...? What's funny in Japan?

It's a private school, and the students must be happy to come, otherwise they might ask their parents to send them somewhere else. Which means that — apart from being a teacher — I must also be an entertainer of sorts.

The two boys run towards me. *"Bei-koku jin!"* they yell. - An American! One of them grabs my leg.

I need to be funny now. But how? Like Matt Dillon in Gunsmoke, I pull an imaginary colt from my hip and fire a couple of shots.

Silence.

At first, I think I did something wrong, but then the boys imitate me and also fire shots in the air.

Tanaka, the head of the tutoring school, is behind the reception desk. He is short and stocky and has rosy cheeks. "May I ask your nationality? It's for our statistics."

The schools only want native speakers, so I have to tweak it a bit.

"USA."

"USA?"

"Yes."

Tanaka presses his tongue between his lips and scribbles a few Japanese characters on a form. "Previous employment?"

I give him the names of a few schools. The boss of the temp agency told me that this would come up. In reality, it's my first job as an English teacher.

I step into the classroom: twenty tables but only two students – the two boys who just exchanged gunshots with me. Quite a surprise. I expected an entire class. The first student has a bob haircut and didn't bother to take of his rain jacket. The other one wears a T-shirt that reads *Tokyo Tigers*.

I have them open their books and let them do a reading exercise: "Jim, Peter and Mary live in San Francisco."

The lesson is a bit awkward. I don't really know what to do with those two youngsters. Their ability to speak English is practically zero. Besides, I have the feeling that the boss is right behind the door, listening.

I had planned to hold the class entirely in English, but it's impossible. I need to speak Japanese to give some basic instructions. Strangely enough, it almost turns into a language class for *me* since the two youngsters start correcting my spotty Japanese.

After what feels like an eternity, I somehow manage to get through with the class and head back to Tokyo.

"How did it go?" Mr. Clean asks.

"Don't know yet."

I take off his tie. "Thank you."

I prepare dinner in the kitchen of the guest house. The ten-year-old son of the owner is playing with a remote-controlled fire engine. The car bumps against my feet.

In the community room, two Argentinians are watching TV: an annoying game show. The guest house is small, and the walls are thin. You can hear pretty much everything the others do.

My "room" is six by six feet and four feet high. I cannot stand up, only sit. It's not a room, really, but more like a coffin since I don't have a window either.

Monthly rent: $500. It's impossible to find something cheaper in Tokyo. The real estate market is absolutely crazy.

The next day.

I take the subway to Shimbashi. Got a call from Inaba, the head of the temp agency. He wants me to fill in for a private lesson because one of the teachers is sick.

Inaba's agency is on the second floor of a grey office building. A sign on the door reads: *Future Communication Center* in English. An interesting name.

I tried to figure out the concept, but it's not entirely clear. Is he trying to say that you can learn here how to communicate in the future? If so, it would be a tricky thing, since we don't really know how people will communicate in the future.

Inaba's agency specializes in language courses. But apparently, he did not get expert advice on the name of his agency. I suppose it's a translation error. What he's trying to say is something like *Modern Communication Center* as opposed to some antiquated language schools that are not really up to date.

The agency consists of a lobby and two small classrooms. Inaba dispatches language teachers to tutoring schools but also offers private courses on site.

Inaba, sitting behind a cluttered desk, sports a

combover and blue-tinted aviator glasses. He points to the classroom. "The student arrived already. Advanced. And always remember: Be funny!"

I step into the classroom. Haruko is twenty-five and works in a bank. She is a bit chubby and has a large gap between her upper incisors. She tells me that she studies English "just for fun." I decide to start with casual conversation.

"Do you like dancing?"
"Oh, yes", Haruko giggles. "I love dance. Can ask where come from?"
"USA."
"USA?"
"Yes."
"You like Eruvisu Puresury?"
"Pardon?"

"Eruvisu Puresury. You not know?"

At once, a light bulb goes off. The Japanese have huge problems with double consonants and with the "L" and the "R" sound. Sometimes you need to take an educated guess from context. She means Elvis Presley, of course.

"Yes, yes sure", I say. "Eruvisu Puresury – the King of Rock'n'Roll."
"Lovu me tenoderu", Haruko says.
"Love me tender?"
"You can sing?"

I remember Inaba's words: *Be funny!* — I'm not really a great singer, but the paying student is king. Fortunately, "Love me Tender" is not that hard, so I just give it a go. I spread my arms, throw my head back and sing a bit exaggerated:

Love me tender, love me sweet
Never let me go
You have made my life complete
And I love you so ...

Haruko giggles again. I notice that the door is slightly open. Inaba listens in!

Somehow, I get the feeling that the Japanese only take English classes because they want to see a foreigner struggle. Who pays, calls the shots, and who is needy must play the part of the dancing bear.

After the lesson with Haruko is over, I want Inaba to pay me out. He also owes me the money for the Yokohama job. Never heard back from the tutoring school. I wasn't funny enough, I guess.

"Payday is on the first," Inaba says, pointing to the calendar. "Today is the 28th."

"Can I get an advance? Kind of tight at the moment."

Inaba looks at his secretary. "How much do we have in the box?"

The secretary opens a drawer and takes out a thin bundle of banknotes which is held together with a paper clip. Inaba counts the money under his desk. He gives me a 10,000 yen note – about a hundred bucks.

The next day.

The locker room in the public pool is neat and quiet. Soft instrumental music emanates from speakers embedded in the ceiling.

Several Japanese men are changing silently and put their belongings very carefully into the lockers, as if there's a sleeping baby nearby they don't want to wake.

As I undress, I notice furtive looks. Most Japanese are curious about a foreigner's endowment in the nether regions.

Today's my big day. I don't earn enough with Inaba's sporadic jobs, so I applied for something completely different: Tonight, I will start working as a male host at a Roppongi night club.

It's a first for me, but I imagine that it will be kind of cool. You chat with Japanese ladies, dance with them, guzzle free drinks and get paid for your time. If I do my job well, Shima will hire me. That's why I'm at the pool. After swimming, I tend to look crisp.

At the entrance to the pool, I need to pass through a knee-high water basin. Automatically, substantial water jets spray at me from left and right. A car wash for humans! Seems to be a safety measure for hygiene.

It's impossible to get to the pool without having showered first.

The pool is packed and rather large. Olympic size. There's not a single foreigner, except me.

I check out some Japanese women and imagine that tonight, I will probably dance and flirt with one or two of them. I decide not to eat any more today. At most, I will drink some tea. I simply look better on an empty stomach!

As I set my foot in the water to swim a lap, I hear a whistle and an announcement in Japanese by megaphone:

"Gai-jin san — Mr. Foreigner, please come to the lifeguard!" Then again: "Mr. Foreigner, please come to the lifeguard!"

This is obviously meant for me, so I get out of the water. The lifeguard sits on an elevated platform. He points at my neck. At first, I don't understand what he means, but then I get it: I must take off my necklace as a safety measure.

Okay, fine. I take off the necklace and put it in my locker. Returning to the pool, I have to pass through the car wash again.

I'm back in the water for maybe ten seconds when I hear an announcement that I don't understand. In a flash, the pool is empty. I'm the only one still paddling around.

The life guard grabs his megaphone: *"Gay-jin san* — Mr. Foreigner, please leave the pool!"

I get out and settle down on a side bench. Some people do gymnastics next to the pool. I ask my neighbor what's going on. He crosses his index fingers. *"Yasumi!"* – Break!

Each full hour, there's a five-minute mandatory break – a safety measure to avoid overexertion.

After the five minutes are up, we get back into the water. Gradually, more people come in, and the pool fills up to the brim. Still, everything remains under control: The lanes are separated by buoys, and you must stay in your lane.

Unfortunately, there are so many people that you have to stand in line at the beginning of the lane. Then, you can swim for about thirty feet until you bump into the line on the other end. The routine goes like this: Swim thirty feet, wait in line for five minutes, swim thirty feet, wait in line for five minutes …

The water in the pool just reaches up to the belly button. Safety measure. Drowning is virtually impossible.

Eight p.m.

I take the elevated subway line to the nightclub in Roppongi. The train is packed with a dressed-up weekend crowd. It smells of deodorant. Neon lights are flickering all around town.

I check out the women in my vicinity: Two office ladies in their early twenties, a woman in her mid-forties with a hat and an older lady in a *kimono*. What type of woman will appear in that night club? And what exactly am I supposed to do?

When I get off in Roppongi, I steer toward the downward lane. The station is so crowded that the stairs are divided by a hand rail into *up* and *down*. Without this division, chaos would reign. It's an impressive picture: In front of me hundreds of Japanese are walking down the stairs. Since they all have black hair, it creates a black wave.

Tokyo by night

The streets in Roppongi are teeming with people. The entertainment district is brightly lit by neon signs.

Passing an amusement arcade, I hear the rattle of *pachinko* balls. *Pachinko* is a pinball machine where you can win prizes. It's extremely popular, and there's a *pachinko* hall on almost every corner in Tokyo.

The night club is called "Outline" and somewhat

run-down. The covers of the side benches have burn holes, but in the dark it's barely noticeable. Most hostess clubs in Tokyo are for men only. "Outline," on the other hand, is for a mixed crowd. That's why they need a male host.

There are no guests, yet. On the side bench next to the entrance, some dressed up Asian women are lined up. They are not from Japan but from Korea, Thailand and the Philippines.

In the far corner of the club, the boss is flipping through a magazine. He looks up and signals for me to come close.

Shima takes a drag on his cigarette. Smoking is still allowed in some Japanese nightclubs if you have a permit. He's wearing a beige jacket and loafers without socks. His eyes seem cold. Lizard eyes.

He makes me rotate in a circle and checks my fingernails. He shakes his head. "No good." He gives me a nail file. "You need a better manicure!"

I head to the bathroom and manicure my fingernails. I barely started, and Shima already gets on my nerves... But I need the money.

The first guest comes in. A woman. The hostesses and I have to line up by the door. The woman is in her early thirties and works in advertising. A regular customer. She sports a washed-out denim jacket and seems pretty cool.

Shima hangs on her every word and laughs constantly. He waves me over.

"A new guy. You like him?"

The woman examines me and takes a drag on her cigarette.

"You like to dance with him?" asks Shima.

"Maybe later."

A group comes in. Two women and four guys. The guys are pretty drunk. One of them wears his necktie as a headband, and his colleague has turned his coat around, so it looks like he's in a straitjacket. The third one has rolled up his pants to above the knees and walks barefoot. Having knotted the laces, his shoes are dangling around his shoulders. They think it's terribly funny and constantly giggle.

And then, the inevitable happens. Shima wants me to sing "My way." Not exactly part of my repertoire, but I can't get around it. Karaoke is a national sport in Japan.

The lyrics of the song flicker in front of me on a screen, and I hammer it out as best I can. After a while I get more confident and crank it up a bit:

And though mistakes I've made a few,
I did it myyyy way ...!

To my surprise, I get applause. Maybe I wasn't so bad after all.

One of the hostesses, a pretty Thai woman, sits on the lap of the guy with the tie headband. She caresses his chin and drags him to the dance floor. The other hostesses also dance with the guests.

Shima motions towards me: *Go ahead!*

I dance with the short, chubby one. She has a golden ribbon in her hair, giggles all the time and asks if I work at the club. Her friend wears a conservative blue costume. She's more on the timid side.

I take turns dancing with the two of them. Both are a bit off the beat. I can't blame them since dancing is not really part of Japanese culture. And if you don't get rhythm early on in life, you might never catch it. So, we hop around a bit and make conversation. The ladies went to the same school and work in a department store. They even know each other as far back as kindergarten. In their spare time, they play tennis and tend to spend their annual vacation together. Preferably in a resort with a tennis court.

Their male colleagues also know each other from kindergarten. Except that they don't play tennis but baseball. In the same club, of course. They are all in their early twenties and still single.

I sense that both women are going for the guy with the necktie headband. I seems that he's a department manager.

The pretty Thai girl and the guy with the headband play Rock, Paper, Scissors. Whoever loses has to hand in a piece of clothing. The guy is pretty drunk and loses almost every time. He's already half naked while the Thai girl has only taken off her bracelet. Eventually, he's down to his briefs.

They shake their fists again, and the guy shows "paper." The Thai girl has "scissors." Now the guy would have to take off his briefs.

The chubby one with the golden ribbon in her hair yells: "The moment of truth, it's here!"

She wants to pull down the guy's briefs, but he's holding her back. "Not you, not you!"

The Thai girl gently pushes the chubby one aside. "Excuse me, but I won the prize!" She takes a glass ashtray and puts it with the opening on top of the briefs, right over the guy's private parts. She taps with the knuckle of her finger on the bottom of the ashtray, as if she wanted to listen if it was hollow behind. The crowd laughs. She plants a kiss on the bottom of the ashtray, leaving the mark of her red lips.

The crowd applauds and yells: *"Ichi ban!"* – Great! The guy puts the ashtray into his jacket as a souvenir.

I head to the bathroom and check my reflection in the mirror. I've hardly eaten all day and feel terribly sick. At once, the Thai girl is next to me. "Come back in! If you stay away too long, you won't get any money."

I'm back on the street. Didn't even say good-bye, just took off. It's cold, and I'm freezing. Still, the fresh air does me good. I loosen the tie, undo the top button of my shirt and take a sigh of relief.

The subway is closed, and a cab is out of the question. Way too expensive. I roughly know where I am and decide to walk home.

Some drunks stagger down the street. One of them sings a Japanese marching tune. In front of a noodle shop, the owner cleans the sidewalk with a water jet from a hose.

My walk home is taking longer than expected. After half an hour, I only covered about a third of the distance. My feet hurt, and I take a break. It's a dark, deserted area. Trucks drive by on an elevated highway.

I notice abandoned bicycles all around me. Some are not locked and have probably been sitting in the same spot for weeks or even months. There's garbage in the baskets.

In Japan, all bikes are registered with the police, and it's easy to find out who's the legitimate owner. Therefore, most bikes are stolen for just one ride and then abandoned. You can see them all around town. Nobody collects them. There are simply too many.

I spot a dusty bike that has garbage in the basket. It's not locked, and there's still air in the tires. My feet hurt from all that walking, so what the heck …

I've hardly mounted the bike when some headlights come on behind me. There's an announcement through a loudspeaker. *"Gay-jin san.* – Mr. Foreigner, this is the police. Stop and get off the bike!"

Tokyo patrol car

Two policemen get out of their patrol car and come towards me. They were parked right behind me in the dark, just waiting for me to take the bike.

They escort me to the station. It's just few hundred yards away. The chief is about sixty and has grey hair. On his desk are small figurines of *sumo* wrestlers and some tattered *manga* – Japanese comic books.

When he hears what happened, he gives me a stern look. As a foreigner, you can get into a lot of trouble for theft. He asks what I do and why I speak Japanese. That's unusual for a foreigner.

I explain that I took a language course at the university.

They give me a cup of tea.

"What were you thinking, Mr. Foreigner?" the chief says. "A young man with a university education … You can ruin your life with something like this!"

I say that I recognize my mistake, but that I was lost and exhausted and that I'll never do it again.

The two officers who arrested me take me home in the patrol car. They want to know my blood type. In Japan, there's a study which attributes the economic success of the Germans and the Japanese to the fact that the majority of people have blood type "A."

I don't even know my blood type and say "zero."
"Blood type zero?"
"Yes."
The guy turns around. "Me and my colleague got type A."

Back in the *Gai-jin House*, I slump onto my *futon*. I'm right above the community room and of course, some roommate has to watch TV in the middle of the night.

There's a knock on my sliding door: Mr. Clean with a bottle of Suntory Whisky, the Japanese national brand. He has just shaved his head, and it shines in the light of the naked light bulb.

We have a shot of whiskey, and Mr. Clean raves about Japan again. Compared to Nigeria, he's doing pretty well here, and because he sends money home every month, he's now the king over there.

He wants to know if I've met a hot girl in the night club. I tell him that it didn't go exactly as planned.

"As a foreigner, you must be funny," Mr. Clean says. "Have you tried being funny?"

"Kind of."
"Okay, but maybe you weren't funny enough ..."

He's probably right. I just wasn't funny enough.

GOOD FOR YOUR KARMA

Question:
How can I make the world a little better?

Answer:
By leaving a customer review for this book! A few clicks, and your karma will improve instantly.

As a small token of appreciation, you will receive The World Is My Oyster (Volume 2) for free.

Here's how it works:
1) Write a customer review on Amazon.
2) Send an email to: info@da-publishing.com with the headline of the review.
3) You will receive your free eBook.

A star rating without a review is also helpful. You won't receive a free book, but it improves your karma as well!

The author learns how to build a house in a Brazilian favela, discovers the secrets of the border wall in Tijuana and gets in trouble with the Russian Mafia in Moscow.

He survives a food poisoning in Cairo, goes celebrity hunting in L.A. and reenacts the fireplace scene of 'The Name of the Rose' in a German monastery.

He experiences in New Jersey that Jewish chicken soup is good for the soul, learns that a spliff is part of breakfast in Jamaica and is admitted to an emergency room in Berlin with a severe head wound.

THE WORLD IS MY OYSTER

VOLUME 3

TRAVELOGUES
MATTHIAS DRAWE

The author discovers the secrets of Buddha's tooth in Sri Lanka, examines the chamber pot of Louis XIV in Versailles and survives a gas leak during Carnival in Rio.

He guzzles a Singapore Sling right at the bar where it was invented, gets robbed in Miami and runs from the police in Quito.

He learns that the life of a New York stand-up comedian is not necessarily funny, discovers why you should never go to Milan in August and finds unexpected love in Ashland (Kentucky).

Printed in Great Britain
by Amazon

50906672R00096